# MIND MAPPING

A Guide to Improve Communication and Time Management

(Time Management and Improve Your Focus in Everyday Life)

**Caitlyn Carr**

Published by Sharon Lohan

© **Caitlyn Carr**

All Rights Reserved

*Mind Mapping: A Guide to Improve Communication and Time Management (Time Management and Improve Your Focus in Everyday Life)*

ISBN 978-1-990334-61-0

All rights reserved. No part of this guide may be reproduced in any form without permission in writing from the publisher except in the case of brief quotations embodied in critical articles or reviews.

Legal & Disclaimer

The information contained in this book is not designed to replace or take the place of any form of medicine or professional medical advice. The information in this book has been provided for educational and entertainment purposes only.

The information contained in this book has been compiled from sources deemed reliable, and it is accurate to the best of the Author's knowledge; however, the Author cannot guarantee its accuracy and validity and cannot be held liable for any errors or omissions. Changes are periodically made to this book. You must consult your doctor or get professional medical advice before using any of the suggested remedies, techniques, or information in this book.

Upon using the information contained in this book, you agree to hold harmless the Author from and against any damages, costs, and expenses, including any legal fees potentially resulting from the application of any of the information provided by this guide. This disclaimer applies to any damages or injury caused by the use and application, whether directly or indirectly, of any advice or information presented, whether for breach of contract, tort, negligence, personal injury, criminal intent, or under any other cause of action.

You agree to accept all risks of using the information presented inside this book. You need to consult a professional medical practitioner in order to ensure you are both able and healthy enough to participate in this program.

# Table of Contents

INTRODUCTION .................................................................. 1

CHAPTER 1: MIND MAPPING ESSENTIAL FUNDAMENTALS 4

CHAPTER 2: ORGANIZE THOSE THOUGHTS! ...................... 10

CHAPTER 3: PURPOSES OF MIND MAPS .......................... 14

CHAPTER 4: TYPES AND EXAMPLES OF MIND MAPPING .. 23

CHAPTER 5: THE POWER OF MIND MAPPING ................... 47

CHAPTER 6: THE WRITER'S BLOCK ..................................... 60

CHAPTER 7: MIND MAPPING PROCESS ............................. 67

CHAPTER 8: HOW TO USE A MIND MAP ........................... 73

CHAPTER 9: BUILDING MIND MAPS THE RIGHT WAY ...... 79

CHAPTER 10: STUDYING AND NOTE TAKING WITH MIND MAPS .......................................................................... 84

CHAPTER 11: HOW TO DESIGN A MIND MAP—OBSTACLES AND CHALLENGES ........................................................... 88

CHAPTER 12: GENERAL BENEFITS ..................................... 94

CHAPTER 13: BENEFITS OF USING A MIND MAP .............. 99

CHAPTER 14: WHY MIND MAPPING? ............................. 106

CHAPTER 15: HOW TO TEACH YOUR CHILDREN MIND MAPPING ......................................................................... 110

CHAPTER 16: MIND MAPPING TECHNIQUES .................. 115

CHAPTER 17: USING COLORS .......................................... 128

**CHAPTER 18: UNLEASH YOUR IMAGINATION WITH MIND MAPPING** ........................................................................ 145

**CHAPTER 19: TECHNIQUES USED IN MIND MAPPING** .... 156

**CHAPTER 20: MANAGING YOUR DAILY LIFE** ................... 179

**CONCLUSION** .................................................................. 192

## Introduction

In the following pages I am about to show you, in the quickest and easiest way possible how you can master the art of mind mapping and use it to improve your life in all areas! Whether you wish to improve your studies, plan projects or simply organise your home life and 'to do' lists then this book will help you get it done, fast.

Mind maps and mind mapping are the best way to organise information as you can see everything at a glance, but more than this, your brain has better recall of details due to the visual nature of mind-mapping. This is the reason that your studying and project management can really improve when you master mind maps.

However, getting the art of mind mapping down to the way that is most helpful to you can be confusing. This is why I wrote this book, to take any of the confusion of headaches away when creating effective and useful mind maps.

Once you master using mind maps you will see marked improvements in your learning, concentration, memorizing, organization, presentations, brainstorming, problem solving, thinking, summarizing, planning, writing, creativity and much more!

Everything in this book is in a simple, easy to understand, step by step manner that you will be able to follow very quickly. I take you from basic mind mapping through to advance techniques that will really improve your workflow.

After reading this book you will be able to organise your life much better – in all areas! There are no limits to how and when you can use a mind map so organising your finances, planning a holiday, running your business, managing your DIY projects, writing a book, revising for an exam and so much more, all become child's play when you use a mind map correctly…

And that is exactly what I want to show you in the next few pages, so without any further ado, let's get started!

# Chapter 1: Mind Mapping Essential Fundamentals

Art Of Mind Mapping

Over the past ten years, researchers have found many advanced understandings for the workings of the human mind. We have a much larger storage reservoir for information and data then once thought, plus a seemingly immeasurable ability to comprehend and think quickly. These updated findings prove that the minds facility to think quickly and effectively is closely related to our imagination and our capacity to produce associations between portions of information.

According to multiple studies about how the brain works, specifically how the mind gathers and stores information, what we learn is automatically stored away in our memory for later retrieval. One researcher visualized this storage system as something similar to many large office file cabinets lined up in the back of the brain containing every fact she had ever come across in her life; and new information is constantly being filed away every day.

How the Brain Works

Much like the rest of the body which comes in pairs, the brain has two parts a left and a right which are called hemispheres and each side executes a different function than the other. The right hemisphere works along the lines of processing visual data and activities. The left hemisphere works on processing analytical information collected from the right side.

An example of the right hemisphere at work would be when you look at something and the information is processed to allow you to say "I know that...that is a dog," or "I know that...that is a swimming pool," or "that's a meatloaf" and so on. The right hemisphere organizes and groups data together.

An example of the left hemisphere at work would be taking the visual data from the right hemisphere and processing it further by adding knowledge and language to it. "Oh, that's Frank's dog Brownie," or "Gail's meatloaf is always moist and delicious" and so on.

The Left Brain

According many studies conducted on the left-brain, right-brain theory, the left hemisphere of the brain is most adept at responsibilities which involve analytical thinking, logic and language.

The left side of the brain is better at:

Reasoning, logic, facts

Practical, safe

Language

Analyzing, ordering, recognizing patterns, sequences

Sciences

Anything dealing with numbers, measurements, math, finances

Critical thinking

The Right Brain

Similar studies and research conducted on the right hemisphere of the brain concluded this side of the brain excels in creative and expressive responsibilities.

The right side of the brain is better at:

Music

Imagination

Imagining the possibilities, the "what-ifs" in life

Expressing emotions, reading emotions

Recognizing faces

Goes beyond the details to see the "big picture"

Creativity

Colors, spatial perception, images

Intuition, feelings

Using Both Sides of Your Brain


Using both the left and right hemispheres of our brain is not difficult; we do it every day, all day long. We make decisions based on what the right side "sees" and then use the logic of the left side of our brain to complete a task. For example, the right side of our brain would process the view of a red stove burner and the left side of our brain would take that information further and turn it into the actionable data which tells us the red stove burner is HOT and DO NOT TOUCH. A lot of the whole brain thinking helps keep us safe and alive like this example.

When you use mind mapping techniques, you are engaging both the right and the left sides of your brain. Although there are no "fast and firm" rules to mind mapping, to achieve the best results, you should use a combination of text, colors, images and shapes. This mixture will appeal to both sides of your brain and help you explore the unusual using your imagination (from the right side) and the ordering and connecting with reasoning (from the left side) will help you solve problems easier.

# Chapter 2: Organize Those Thoughts!

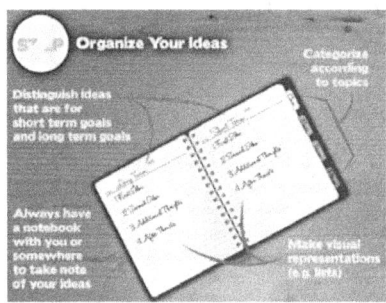

It is not enough to remember your thoughts and ideas. In fact the reason why you are reading this book is to organize those thoughts right? Organizing your thoughts requires discipline and consistency. Once you forget to do one thing a lot or even everything could go wrong. This step might seem to be a bit of a hassle but it is also important to success.

Tip 1: Always Have a Notebook With You For Notes

This sounds pretty simple right? Well quite honestly it is not. There are a lot of things that can make you forget to bring a notebook and a pen. One of them is laziness. You will always feel like bringing a notebook is useless because you can remember things anyway and it will only be one extra thing to carry around. That's just your lazy self talking! We have established that writing things down is better than taking note using gadgets so bring a notebook and a pen all the time. You won't regret it. It's better to be safe than sorry, you never know when a good idea might suddenly pop into your head.

Tip 2: Distinguish Ideas that are for Short Term Goals from Ideas for Long Term Goals

Now that you have your ideas written down and you can remember them it is important to know which ideas are for short term goals and which are for long term goals. Why is this? Well this will surely help with efficiency. It will be better to focus on the ideas which need to be used earlier and put aside ideas that will not be used yet so that you will not get confused. By focusing on the "now" you will be able to finish tasks faster.

Tip 3: Categorize Your Thoughts According to Topic

We all have our limitations both physically and mentally, we just cannot do everything all at the same time. It is quite literally impossible. This is why it is important to categorize the ideas and thoughts that you will be using. Throughout the day there is a time for work, for relaxation, for hobbies, for friends, family etc. Categorizing your thoughts will help you focus on the task at hand and be more efficient in utilizing those thoughts and ideas to your benefit. For example when you are at work you will only need to think about work related ideas which increases productivity.

Tip 4: (Again Write it Down!) Make lists

Another use for your notebook is further organizing your ideas and thoughts by making lists. Now that you have categorized them according to topic and you have already distinguished which ideas need to be given priority you will be prepared to make lists. As mentioned earlier the physical reminders help you focus better and remember better. Using the work example mentioned in the previous tip you can see how it will be more beneficial and efficient to write things down and put them in lists. This will also help you develop discipline and good character which can help you in a lot of things.

## Chapter 3: Purposes Of Mind Maps

Mind Maps can be described simply as a tool to help man organize his clutter. Most of our day-to-day activities, planned as they might be, are often bombarded by unexpected events. When these inevitable surprises come upon our way, we are often thrown off course. We become disorganized and we tend to lose focus. Mind mapping techniques can be very useful for many things. Below are some points to consider why you need to have Mind Mapping in your life:

For figuring things out

When you are thinking through complicated problems, you need to be able to find a semblance of order. You will be, without a doubt, distracted by your emotions and that's a normal human reaction to expect. You will be anxious, worried and even restless. Most of the time, you will find it hard to think things through. The likelihood of you making rushed decisions will be very high. Oftentimes, you'd just want to get it over with.

Having a Mind Map at hand will somehow remind you to take a step back and to take a good look at the real "shape" of the problem at hand. Going through the process will force you, in a good way, to search your brain for new ideas and alternative options.

It will show you that there might be other ways for you to resolve your problems. It will help you figure out which will be the best route to take. And if that doesn't work, then you'll be able to quickly pick out your plan B. A Mind Map will also allow you to see your problem as it is. By putting it on paper, affirming and acknowledging its existence and presence in your life.

And once you do that, you are able to properly assess and evaluate how it would actually affect you. Sometimes, the worries and apprehensions are all in our minds. Once you have it all laid out in front of you, you might surprise yourself when you realize that it's not that big of a problem at all.

For brainstorming and bouncing ideas

Whether you are by yourself, with a friend or colleagues, you will often find yourself mulling things over. You are a thinking human being therefore, it is inevitable for your mind to ask questions and come up with ideas. More often than not, you'd find yourself bouncing of ideas with other people until you have with you a long list of brilliant ideas. Once you have all them written down, what then are you going do with them?

Mind Mapping can help you classify these seemingly random thoughts for them to make sense. Individually, each idea seemed amazing but as a whole, it may seem like they won't work. Don't lose hope. Maybe you just need to lay them all out there in the open and with the help of

Mind Mapping techniques, connect the dots until they make sense.

For consolidating thoughts and ideas that are all over the place

The mind is a very active organ. It is constantly running and churning out ideas. It is so active that sometimes, we find ourselves flooded with too much information that we end up feeling overwhelmed and confused. Mind Mapping can help consolidate these ideas for them to make sense. It is common for us to think of various solutions to a certain problem that sometimes, we end up not resolving anything. Our thoughts are all over the place. We want to do so many things all at the same time that we end up not being able to finish any of the tasks we intended to do in the first place.

For summarizing everything and getting to the bottom of it all

Mind mapping can help you get the gist of the tons and tons of information that you've gathered. Once you are able to lay out everything and are able to connect the dots, you will be able to get a better picture of what it is that you truly want to achieve. There are times when we become too focused on the details that we forget to look at the bigger picture.

Having a Mind Map will allow you to actually see where the different ideas will take you, what you need to make them work and what are the possible consequences and potential threats for each of them. You will be able to realize that no matter how many paths you take, no matter how many steps or processes you follow, all roads will still lead you to your goal—your core or central idea.

For studying and learning it all

We often find our minds turning into mush whenever we are studying for an exam. This is because we often end up overloading our brains with information that we ought to have learned over a longer period of time. Mind Mapping techniques can help streamline the tons and tons of information and data that we are feeding our brains.

It can help us make sense of the tons of information we've read from books or those that we've gathered from research and classroom discussions. When we create a Mind Map from what we've heard or read, we end up creating a visual representation of everything that we've learned. When we have a mental image of all our lessons, it becomes easier for us to recall certain topics especially during exams when we are oftentimes not allowed to check our books or notes for reference.

For enticing presentations

Having a Mind Map can help you create visually entertaining and informative presentations! You can actually use your Mind Map as the presentation itself. It is easier to follow the flow of thoughts and ideas when the audience are presented with an entire page showing the actually "shape" and "picture" of the subject or topic that they are representing. Contrary to what most people believe in, that readers tend to scan or read from left to right and from top to bottom, many actually tend to look at a page presented to them in a non-linear manner.

Mind Maps also employ the use of imagery, catchy words, and colors. These are very visual representations of a person's ideas that can easily catch someone's attention. When you employ all these factors in your presentation, you are guaranteed to capture your audience therefore allowing you to effectively and clearly communicate the message that you want to convey.

For planning ahead

Mind Maps can give you the ability to forecast the future. The tree-like diagram allows you to see where the arrows are headed. When you can see at a glance your projected glide path, it is easier for you to determine your progress. You will be able to tell if you are moving towards the right direction or if you need to do some modifications with your plans. Seeing potentials threats and obstacles lay out in front of you will also allow you to anticipate what might happen. This will enable you to prepare and create counter measures that will help you avoid those pitfalls.

For your peace of mind

Mind Maps can actually give you peace of mind. Yes, you read that right my friend. Mind Mapping can actually bring you peace of mind. When your mind is too busy generating new ideas you may find yourself overwhelmed and inundated with tons and tons of information. These can cause you to worry too much. Anxiety can lead to stress and stress can have an awful effect on your body. When your mind is noisy all the time, you deny yourself the ability to hear the sounds that truly matter. You are unable to hear the callings of your soul, the voice of your heart and most of all, the callings of the Universe.

Having a Mind Map will allow you to rid your mind of all the noise and chaos. It will enable you to transfer the thoughts that are flooding your mind, to paper. You will be able to lay out everything in front you. Your thoughts will not just remain as thoughts. You will be able to see them for what they are. You will be able to assess them and find out if they will actually work once you implement them in the real world. Your mind will be relieved and you will find stillness inside you.

# Chapter 4: Types And Examples Of Mind Mapping

As brain maps are widely utilised in both private life and functioning, it's vital for everybody to be aware of the basic kinds of thoughts maps, so they can decide on an appropriate one to use. Fundamentally, mind maps can be broken into 3 classes based on the objective of utilizing: library thought maps, demonstration mind maps and tube deadline thought maps. We'll elaborate on them later.

Mind maps are widely utilized by both designers and non-designers as a way of brainstorming in the first phases of jobs to be able to explore ideas or resolve project issues. In an earlier article, we explored the idea of mind maps and how to use them by beginning with a core idea and expanding it into a tree structure, to link thoughts and elaborate these thoughts into more information. Mind maps can be made using drawing paper or a white board, utilizing post-it sticky notes, or utilizing online tools. Our designer mind map template contains printing components that may be utilised in building flexible brain maps.

As brain maps are widely utilized in staff meetings, attaining a thriving mind mapping session necessitates understanding the various kinds of brain maps and which is an appropriate fit throughout the meeting. Normally, there are 3 common kinds of brain maps depending on the projects' function: library thought maps are utilized to monitor data, demonstration mind maps are utilized to present thoughts, and tube timeline thought maps are utilized to arrange and construct a project strategy. This taxonomy is regarding the goal of using mind maps as well as the sort of information employed from the brainstorming session.

Mind maps are mainly utilized at the early phase of a project or application to research the topic or resolve problems. In accordance with different functions, mind maps could be classified into 3 types:

Library head maps for advice organizing

Presentation thought channels for presenting ideas and jobs

Tunnel deadline thought maps for arranging or creating a job plan

#mind map form 1: library mind maps

Library mind maps are also known as reference maps. This sort of head map is primarily utilized to arrange information, so you are able to have a clear understanding of the issue without missing anything. The objective of library thought maps would be to sort and arrange the gathered information for a better comprehension of the subject.

Library mind maps, also known as the reference maps, are utilized to organize information visually, so several pieces of advice or themes could be viewed easily without sacrificing any component. So this mind map begins with a variety of broken thoughts or themes, then these thoughts are coordinated together in a tree structure. This arrangement tends to construct a linkage between related thoughts and arrange the way the most important topics intersect. The library map concentrates on the notion, so it begins with the most important thought, and it directs the brainstorming session by following the associated subjects into the center ideas.

After developing a library mind map, the first step would be to place all the information together and arrange it into a map shrub. The map will reveal how every piece is connected to each other and how they could serve the principal thought.

This sort of mind map may be utilized for organizing information about a particular subject in a visual manner; below are a few examples: personal profile mind map

The library mind map may be accustomed to reach these:

Research a particular subject and the associated thoughts around it. By way of instance, team members can use this procedure to research a particular issue, like a traffic light and each of the issues associated with the problem so as to resolve it.

Organize information about a particular job or subject within a visual method, which may be readily tracked during the conversation.

# mind map type 2: display mind maps

This sort of mind map is accustomed to present the practice of a concept to your audience. Demo mind maps illustrate the manner in which the job goes so as to monitor the measures. Therefore, the attention of a demonstration mind map is your audience rather than the topic. How the information ought to be placed from the map is dependent on if the viewer can know it or not. If the audience can follow the way you're displaying, then the map is nicely structured. Thus, your demonstration can be accepted by the viewers.

This kind of thought map is used to present a development of ideas, like telling a narrative or monitoring a call to action procedure. These thoughts maps are inclined to present the notions' stream visually to be able to monitor the measures along with the information related to every measure. Contrary to the reference thought map, the demonstration mind map is made to stick to the dialogue and envision its own particular flow, instead of restraining the session throughout the accumulated thoughts. Therefore, this method targets the attendees instead of the topic. Even though the primary issue is composed as the foundation for the brain map, it's controlled with the group discussion.

This sort of mind map may be accustomed to reach the following:

Map a particular consumer behaviour when utilizing a solution along with the measures that the customer followed as a way to record a particular target, like purchasing a product or subscribing to your site.

Training sessions, even once the trainee should adhere to a particular stream of information. It's a simplified version of a PowerPoint presentation with a more direct and simple strategy.

Discuss a debate or a scenario and the actions based on this circumstance.

This kind of mind map may be utilized for describing an action or a coaching session. Here are the examples: Sunday activities mind map

#mind map form 3: tunnel timeline mind maps

This kind of mind map will also be simplified as planning brain channels. They are primarily used for a job plan, program plan, or problem solving. Tunnel timeline thought maps are made to attain a goal. The objective of this sort of mind map is to picture success. The centre (main subject ) of this brain map is the outcome that you simply pursue, and every sub-topic represents a route to achieve that result. It is possible to follow the map to generate progress to the success.

When preparing for a particular job or choosing from other activities during the project advancement, the preparation mind map may be used to present different activities as well as the connections sub-actions that could be expected from various plans. For instance, this kind of mind map may be used for a particular program, like a job plan, action program, or problem solving. The core subject of this brain map reflects the desirable result. Each sub-topic intends to represent a route that goes toward attaining the core goal. For instance, the core idea can be raising the market share by a particular percent, along with the associated subject focusing on the strategies to attain this objective. These kinds of thought maps may be utilised to attain the next.

Plan jobs and construct a job plan that may be accomplished through specific measures.

Solve issues through placing the hunt for an answer as the primary goal and discussing the probable procedures for solving the issue through the subsequent session.

This sort of mind map may be utilized for planning job plans or solving issues. Here are the examples: marketing plan mind map.

Mind maps can be a strong instrument to research thoughts, build project plans, and resolve problems. The 3 kinds of thought maps mentioned previously can cover virtually all the mind maps. Understanding the qualities and functions of every kind can help you attain the results required with brain maps.

A head map can be a powerful instrument to explore creative ideas, construct strategies, or resolve issues. But lots of mind map sessions are neglected as a result of incorrect implementation for the procedure. To be able to attain a thriving mind-mapping assembly, facilitators should employ the most suitable mind map for attaining the meeting's purpose. The aforementioned three brain maps cover virtually all of the functions where brain maps can be implemented. Knowing the features and the use of every type is necessary to attain the desired results from brain map sessions.

Types of mind maps

Mind mapping is a technique for analyzing issues and developing approaches in a nonlinear manner. Mind-map production uses felt tip pens on flip-chart newspaper, markers on whiteboards or pc mind-mapping computer software. Completed mind maps include phrases, linking arrows, lines and at times drawings. Head maps types involve problem solving, project and understanding.

#problem-fixing maps

A mind map is a useful instrument to utilize during staff brainstorming sessions once the objective is to create ideas quickly, without instant logical review. Displaying the brain map through the semester enables team members to observe the ideas created, which arouses more thoughts. This procedure creates favorable momentum for problem solving.

A difficult brainstorming session begins with the leader recording the issue as a phrase or little picture in the middle of what's going to develop into the brain map. As staff members engage with opinions, the recorder brings coloured spokes radiating from the heart issue. Each spoke represents another part of the matter and can be tagged with a word or graphic. As the session proceeds, the remarks of staff members lead to the inclusion of smaller lines flowing out of the spokes and of arrows demonstrating connections between objects on distinct spokes.

Problem-solving mind maps tend to be utilized only during the brainstorming session. Team members shout out their thoughts, structure the map, set priorities, and make action items. Following the brain map eases this procedure, so it's no more needed. The life spans of mind maps are usually only a couple of hours.

#project maps

Planning an event, planning an item launching, creating the strategy to shut a massive sale, and other actions can create project thought maps. Updated occasionally to reflect changes in job status, they live just until job completion. The life spans of job mind maps are usually only a couple of days or months.

#knowledge maps

Knowledge mind maps include information recorded once and retained for later use, occasionally replacing existing files. Some are fine-tuned and upgraded over time, while some are not upgraded. Mind maps describing business procedures, occasionally including checklists, are cases of understanding mind maps. Used multiple occasions during a very long interval, understanding mind maps are significant in maintaining corporate background, the never-recorded knowledge present only inside the minds of workers. Knowledge mind maps may be especially valuable for new workers in discovering previous procedures for conducting recurring actions. The life spans of understanding mind maps may be years.

How mind map can assist your creative thinking

A mind map is a visual manner of teams to catch, store, and organize ideas. By amassing subtopics within an unordered manner, mind maps make it possible for teams to handle problem solving in a natural manner.

Rather than hard-to-review notice taking or disparate meetings, thoughts maps bring teams together and make it easy to collaborate on a huge array of jobs.

5 kinds of mind maps

There are five kinds of head maps. Straightforward, notion, and arbitrary word thought maps are great for freeform brainstorming among almost any group. Flowcharts and dialog mind maps are used by agile teams spark retrospectives, preparation, along with other job tasks.

1. Simple mind map

A mind map is a visual diagram in the form of a shrub or tree, where important groups radiate from a central node, and lower categories will be the sub-branches of bigger ones.

A mind map is a free default application in miro. It is possible to concentrate on the real thoughts and use only a few hotkeys to construct the map. In addition, with miro, you are able to set images, videos and other visuals beside your brain map to encourage and expand upon your thoughts.

Measures for making your map:

Start at the middle of a blank canvas, giving your mind the freedom to distribute and communicate ideas freely and naturally.

Use colours throughout; it provides additional vibrancy and life to a brain map.

Use one keyword online as it provides your brain map more flexibility and power.

Use pictures throughout. A photo is worth a million words and makes it possible to use your creativity.

2. Concept map

A concept map is a chart used to illustrate the connections between theories at a brainstorming session. An idea is a thought frame defined by an explicit "focus question". Mapped theories represent a hierarchical structure that lets you further understand the issue and build stronger arguments.

A concept map differs in the brain map from the design. Ordinarily, it follows a hierarchical arrangement and reveals more complicated interrelations between theories (a theory may relate to more than only the mother node).

To begin mapping theories, you simply have to concentrate on the ideas. Here's an easy guide to the procedure:

Insert a form or decal with the overall subject you want to know more about. Ensure it is the answer to a specific question.

Brainstorm the listing of topics about the topic. Use bulk-add style for sticky notes to follow your train of thought and retain the concepts as succinct as you can.

Start mapping topics around the idea and then connect them with lines. More significant ideas should be nearer to the middle and less significant ones nearer to the border. Insert text to describe the connections more clearly.

## 3. Random words

Random phrases is a brainstorming technique that motivates your creativity to create unique viewpoints and fresh perspectives on the thought or the problem you're facing. By assessing your surroundings, you develop fresh ideas that could help you resolve the issue.

By forcing yourself to utilize a random word to locate a solution, you're almost sure to go beyond the bounds and attack the issue from another way.

Here is the way to utilize this brainstorming method:

Identify the issue or challenge you're facing.

Using a mind map tool, make the initial node with a random note. This term has to be entirely arbitrary and irrelevant to your issue or challenge.

Applying shortcuts, write down as many ideas as possible that are connected with the arbitrary word.

Using a remark instrument, examine the links between your arbitrary institutions along with your difficulty or challenge. Write down the thoughts that come into mind.

4. Flowchart

A flowchart is an incremental algorithm, workflow or procedure visualized with contours of different varieties and arranged with arrows.

Flowcharts help picture a particular procedure to assist, understand, and detect defects and bottlenecks. There are various kinds of flowcharts, and while a few of them need specific kinds of shapes (such as ovals or diamonds), a very simple sitemap or business procedure will use text boxes.

The best way to make a flowchart:

Kick your thinking process by incorporating the initial product.

Utilize control dots around the first thing to begin drawing on a connection inside your mind mapping applications. You will notice the menu where it is possible to decide on the next thing, producing your thought flow as easily as possible.

Customize the appearance and feel of this flowchart, utilizing item menus for both arrows and objects.

5. Dialogue map

Dialogue mapping is a facilitation technique. The map encourages a shared comprehension of a wicked problem, in which technical and social complexities have been set up.

When a bunch of smart individuals gather to fix a complicated or challenging problem, the frequent question is: how do they see the entire picture and know what the issue truly is? Teams throughout the world can view the large image in actual time and preserve shared knowledge, remote accessibility, and knowledge retainment. The built-in brain mapping tool can help dig into the issue further and brainstorm it quicker.

Dialogue mapping contrasts nicely with agile practices and could be a highly effective instrument to provide focus, clarity and advice to agile actions. It may even be used for retrospective meetings, making a better comprehension of the following improvement to be produced by the agile group, make sure it is scrum, fdd, lean, rup or any development group.

The best way to make a dialog map:

Produce the initial node using all the mind map tools. Begin with a query or an issue. It might be something as straightforward as "agenda?" or as complicated as "what do we do to become much better product programmers?"

Start adding thoughts using shortcuts.

Insert "pro" and "con" arguments to every idea. Highlight positives and drawbacks with various colors using the brain map toolbar.

To solidify mutual comprehension, complete with a list of what's been identified.

Head maps: paper vs virtual

Mind maps are fast replacing lists, summaries, and other linear types of business for an assortment of applications. Almost anyone, such as professionals and students, may benefit from using them in college, work, or perhaps mundane applications like grocery store and to-do lists.

Traditionally, they have been performed using paper and pencil.

The benefit of this method is that this sort of mind map can be performed anywhere, at any moment, and you've got access to it. Additionally, even individuals that are uncomfortable with technology may utilize this method.

The learning procedure is occasionally aided by hand-writing items, and you may add as much colour and as numerous examples as you want to your own map.

Regrettably, hand-drawn ones are not necessarily the optimal solution.

They could tear, get filthy, become lost, plus they just take up space. They take more time to make compared to the virtual one. Virtual ones can be produced with mind mapping applications, of which there's a variety, and possess some benefits over hand-drawn.

They require less time to make, changes could be made easily and inexpensively, they need no physical space to shop, plus they appear more professional.

The sole disadvantage to virtual ones would be that, of course, they need a computer to make, and people occasionally find themselves making a map at home when they wanted to talk with other people on the job, rather than using it there, or even attempting to make a mind map at work but using the applications on their computer.

These issues, however, can be solved using a great mind mapping program.

This lets you create an individual on any pc; that's an excellent benefit if you're doing work-related jobs on both your home and work pcs.

Being able to save the maps you create permits you to start working on a project at work, then finish it in your home or vice versa. Additionally, it lets you make a mind map in your home or in your laptop during a trip or long bus journey, then bring it into work to share with your coworkers.

While conventional, pen-and-paper work equally in addition to virtual ones, such as improving your business and productivity, a lot of men and women are discovering that digital maps are easier to store, arrange and share. You could even make adjustments to some virtual mind maps without making the map cluttered, unlike newspaper.

With all the software available to make brainstorm maps, it is no wonder they're quickly becoming a favorite practice among individuals from all walks of life.

# Chapter 5: The Power Of Mind Mapping

Mind Mapping and Problem Solving

Are you among the individuals who get stressed up whenever you face difficulties over certain situations? For instance, do you find looking for something in your room stressful? Most likely, if you have a disorganized room, you are led to different directions when finding something. However, if you want to change your life in terms of solving both minor and major problems, then you can use mind mapping.

Mind mapping is designed to help you address some, if not all the problems that come up in life. Such problems could be related to personal projects or business ventures among other niches. Mind mapping also allows you to visualize your ideas or tasks, which are often interrelated. Mind maps can help you become more systematic and productive.

Those with school children might have already heard of mind mapping. It is majorly used by school teachers in aiding the children understand a number of lessons. It is also common to find a number of businesses that enjoy using mind mapping during their meetings or sessions. Mind mapping is useful in such cases whenever brainstorming is required to develop new business opportunities or possibilities. Mind mapping is also used for projects that call for immediate action. Through mind mapping, you can come up with solutions to a problem by simply writing down your goals using short words, lines, graphics, and/ or drawings. It would not take long to come up with a solution to your problem or complete a certain project or task.

Those new to mind mapping can make use of online tools in familiarizing themselves on the concepts employed. Given that mind mapping can be difficult for beginners, learning the basics from online tools can be of great help. Many mind mapping websites offer tools that teach and help in creating mind maps. On the other hand, if you are a beginner, it is advisable to create a mind map for personal use first instead of starting with a complex problem, topic, or issue.

It is advisable that you start with your own goals. You might get interested in writing down a vacation plan, a family night or daily household chores. If you are concerned about your health, you can write down vitamins, exercise, and water intake among others. If you have a business, you can include affiliate, articles, website, and newsletter. You can start creating mind maps once you list down all possible links or ideas for a specific topic or issue. Mind mapping involves choosing a central goal or topic and determining other minor goals, which branch out from the central goal.

Mind maps will guide you in discerning the root cause of the problem. This is because you are able to picture how you will prioritize different aspects of your life.

Thus, it could be the start of a more organized living. Mind mapping allows you to plan your goals and act on it appropriately.

In problem solving, mind maps are useful in organizing a number of life aspects as well as discerning the next step of action. It can help you be more productive regardless of the problem you are facing.

Mind Mapping for Everyday Living

Dealing with a huge amount of information on a daily basis is inevitable. If the information gathered on a daily basis is not gathered or classified, it could easily become meaningless. It may also be difficult to sort out information, which usually comes from people, books, abstracts, magazines, websites, and other sources such as video tapes and radio networks. Therefore, if you want to live a much easier life every day, mind mapping is the solution.

Mind maps make it possible for one to assimilate all the information gathered on a daily basis. This is because mind maps help you organize every piece of information by unlocking your brain's fullest potential. All you need is a paper and some colored pencils or markers to create your mind map.

Computer-aided/digital maps are available on the online platform. They operate with a similar concept to that of traditional mind maps. However, their computerized mode helps them yield more results. Digital or computer-aided mind maps also allow you to draw and edit your ideas. More so, you can make use of these mind maps for business conferences or presentations and even share them to a group through the computer and internet.

Mind mapping is definitely useful in your everyday life regardless of whether you are using computer-aided or paper tools. Perhaps you might not be aware that you are already doing mind maps to organize daily ideas through simple drawings, lines, and sketches.

When collecting ideas or information, it is advisable that you write them down instead of recording them in a textual format. Jot down ideas and information in a comprehensible mind map. You will notice that your brain becomes more stimulated. In addition, it can be easier for you to recall your ideas. Through mind maps, the ideas or information you collect can easily be understood with just one look.

Mind Mapping and Your Studies

Studying can often result to an overload in the mind regardless of the age. However, the possibilities of such conditions is minimal especially if one considers good work ethics. Mind mapping can help you organize yourself in order to deal with issues or situations on your studies efficiently through the aid of charts. You can use the diagramming techniques of mind mapping to create charts for note taking as well as concepts. These techniques are very useful in studying as they can help in absorbing or understanding lessons and information. As a result, the outcome is likely to be higher or improved grades as well as a fruitful academic career.

Mind mapping techniques also involve the generation of charts that are beneficial in the development or improvement of study habits. They can help one improve their note-taking skills as well as take less time in organizing and compiling their notes. This is possible since mind mapping charts only have the keyword that is vital to the lesson being studied. Additionally, it is possible to recall a great percentage of information inputted in the mind maps as one studies for the exams or writes an easy. Mind mapping charts are easier to memorize as compared to conventional notes; thus, your grades will improve immensely. These charts are also useful references before taking an exam. You also get to manage your time better through mapping out your strategies for study. For instance, if you are writing essays or academic papers, you can use the diagramming techniques of mind mapping to brainstorm ideas as well as create charts.

Mind mapping techniques allow for the prioritization of study tasks as well as expansion of ideas. Such skills are necessary in helping you improve your study skills. More so, mind mapping techniques can aid you in generating creative ideas, which can be magnified with mind mapping charts and diagrams.

Mind Mapping and Work Performance

Work performance is one of the most important considerations to make whenever you have a job. You can easily benefit from promotions, compensation raises and bonuses is you optimize your work performance in the right manner. Mind mapping can aid you in starting to optimize the efficiency of your work performance . You will be able to brainstorm effectively and organize your time through diagramming techniques.

In order to effectively optimize your work performance, you need to create charts inputted and expanded with your ideas. This can relatively be important during brainstorming since it allows you to contribute excessively in the area of expertise. Mind mapping helps you improve your ability to generate, gather, absorb, and organize information. Your mind map or diagram consisting of singe keywords that represent concepts and tactics can help you understand and recall better. Using charts allows you to prioritize tasks, which in turn optimizes your work efficiency. Moreover, mind mapping can aid you in managing your time better and make you more productive in your job.

Mind mapping is also useful in enhancing the skills of the leaders in the workplace. Using charts, leaders can generate ideas by encouraging theory team members to contribute during the brainstorming session. Members in a team also have the capability to create individual charts that can be integrated at a later stage. Your planning skills can be improved as well given that all potential ideas are already laid. You will be able to plan ahead and have a picture of what you need to do next. With mind mapping, you will be able to analyze situations that will lead to optimizing your work performance. Thus, you can use mind mapping in just about any situation in your workplace.

Mind Mapping and Learning

Those willing to learn as fast as possible can employ mind maps to their advantage. Naturally, college students are always prompted to note down some important points of consideration especially when they are getting ready for an exam or test. Apart from the necessity to focus on daily class discussions, they also need to read and understand their textbooks. There are cases when students go through information overload, which makes it difficult for them to learn.

One of the hardest things to learn in a lesson involving languages is text information. However, mind maps have the capability to guide students in coping up with their studies as well as have better learning skills.

Every individual is definitely unique. Individuals also learn differently from each other. One method for learning could work well for one and not for the other one. Take for example jotting down notes. This method of learning or studying is considered a passive process. The brain does not interact with the information that you are jotting down. Thus, if you want to recall what you have written, your brain should be more interactive and involved.

In the current society, visual learning has become a popular trend in a number of schools as well as universities. Based on recent surveys, students are able to learn better when teachers and professors make use of drawings, graphics, and even cartoons in their methods of teaching.

It can often be easy for visual learners to familiarize themselves with the techniques involved in mind mapping. Learning maps are the tools used in learning and mind mapping. On the other hand, it may be a little hard for beginners to use learning maps although with frequent use, they can master their abilities to create these maps.

Learning maps are also commonly referred to as memory maps. These maps include more of drawings and graphics and less of texts. Many students who use learning maps can recall and retain information more efficiently as compared to those using traditional note-taking.

Mind mapping for learning can often be a useful technique in improving your learning skills as well as habits. However, this depends on your ability or preferences. Just like mind maps used in other areas, learning maps are created using a paper and colored pens/ markers. You start at the middle portion of the paper with your goal and branch out other vital information that you need in your lesson.

Learning maps can still be created during class discussions. This can be made possible by discerning the central idea behind your discussion and noting it down centrally on a piece of paper. On the other hand, avoid using sentences in your diagram. Keywords are the best to use given that you still need to branch out and determine sub ideas of the discussion. Use lines to connect the main idea to the sub ideas until the end of your class discussion.

Learning maps can also be created while reading textbooks. It can be easier to learn from books if you are trying to visual what you are reading. You can do this by creating learning maps.

## Chapter 6: The Writer's Block

In this chapter, we will be focusing on the writer's block. The writer's block is when you have caught in a situation where you cannot anymore think of new ideas and you just lost the creativity to put more in writing your work. This causes you to slow down and sometimes not be able to finish what you are writing about. Therefore it is important that we prevent this from happening or cure yourself of this condition so here are tips on how you can deal with the writer's block:

**Do something creative**. If you can't unleash your creativity, why not stimulate it by doing other creative things aside from writing? Think of the things you usually do to be satisfy your hunger for creativity. If you love dancing, turn up the volume and play your favorite song you love dancing to. Make your favorite dish if you love cooking. If you love drawing and painting, bring your sketchpads or canvass out and spend a little time with your favorite art activity. Whatever that is, pause with your writing and do your creative activity for a while in order to encourage more creative juice out.

**Freewriting**. If you are really stuck at what you are writing about, freewriting is another way to get out of it. Set your timer to a few minutes and start writing about anything. Do not worry about your grammatical correctness, punctuation marks, and the legibility of your handwriting and just write freely. Write what first comes in your head and tell things about it. Write about what you did yesterday, where you went, who you have been with. Just continue writing ideas until the alarm goes off. Do it regularly, maybe every other day or maybe even everyday as part of your routine. This not only maintains your creative state but also the ideas you write can actually be inspiration to what you are writing about and could possibly new ideas for you to include to your article or book.

**Move**. When you are stuck there sitting on your office chair and just staring at a blank page for too long, get up and start moving. Dance to your favorite song. Do your workout. Go out for a jog or run. Do things that will make your body active because when your body becomes active, your brain follows. And when your brain gets activated, you will start to squeeze more creative juice out of it.

**Start early**. When you wake up, you will still be in that phase where you are creative. Why not start your day with your mind map because in doing that, not only will you finish early but also be able to do a good one and you can start your writing right away. For some people, they wake up at 5 in the morning and for others, they wake up at noon. Whatever time of the day you wake up, start it by doing your mind map or resuming to where you last left on what you were writing about.

**Think of your problem before falling asleep**. You are stuck in a particular part of your mind map or whatever you are writing about let's say, a particular chapter of your novel, then your day is about to end without being able to move forward. Think of your problem or the part where you are stuck as you fall asleep. Because as you are sleeping, your mind still subconsciously thinks of your problem and because of that, dreams can be your solution and when you wake up, you will usually have a thing or two in mind as your way to continue with your work. Think of your problem as you lay down in bed and as you close your eyes to sleep and wake up with a solution to it!

**Rest and relax.** When you are too exhausted to function, do not forget to pause and take a nap or go to sleep. It has also been scientifically proven that getting enough sleep will enable your brain to function well and yourself to be more creative. And if you have been staying up late and probably have been lacking on sleep, even the easiest of tasks will be difficult for you so pause for a while and give yourself a good sleep or a short nap if you are running out of time to catch your deadline. When you are running on enough sleep but you really just can't squeeze your creative juice out and you are stressed, give yourself a little break and close your eyes for a while. Breathe deeply and slowly and try o clear your head a little. When you are relaxed, you can allow your mind to open and yourself to be more creative.

**Have a pen and paper ready**. When you are stuck and just gave yourself a break, do not forget to always capture your creative ideas when the moment comes. When you're going out for a workout at the gym, have a pen and paper with you just to be ready because you will never know when that special idea comes. Be ready to record or jot down your own thoughts right there and then.

**Give yourself a meal**. Take care of your health because when you are in perfect shape, it your mind follows it. Eat well and don't skip meals. Start your day with a breakfast. Eat different kinds of food. Have variety and moderation when eating. Just like getting enough rest, your diet is scientifically proven to influence your brain function. So go eat your meal if you are hungry and don't forget to hydrate yourself properly by drinking enough water for the day.

**Learn by reading and listening**. If you are running out of creativity in your writing, you might be needing a few more lessons to learn in order to inspire you and equip you with new and better ideas to write about. Read different materials like the daily newspaper, Hollywood and celebrity news, your favorite magazines, and even the most scientific of textbooks you prefer. Because by reading, you not only learn about the topic they have written on that material, but also be able to widen your vocabulary and improve your writing skills. In addition to that, you might be able to bump into new ideas that you can probably include in what you are writing about. Talk to people and listen to what they have to say, because you might learn something that you will not find in your regular reading materials. Let them talk about their experiences and challenges and how they dealt with these. Do not hesitate to ask and extract the information you need because when you learn, you become more equipped for what you will be writing about.

Idea mapping in itself encourages you to be creative and prevent the writer's block and that is one very important thing to remember here. So aside from focusing on things on how to prevent the writer's block, start doing your idea map and make it fun and memorable.

## Chapter 7: Mind Mapping Process

To start mind mapping all you need is blank piece paper and a pen (colour pens are very useful but not essential) and you're ready to go. Here are a 8 steps to follow when Mind Mapping for clearer thinking.

Step 1: Write down what you want to think about - Write down a word or two of what you want to think about in the centre of the page. Put a circle around it to ensure that it has the focus.

Step 2: Don't over think it - Write down the first things that come up into your mind when you start to think about related issues, people, objects, goals, etc. Put these thoughts around the central thought. These can be anything, even if they look strange or unimportant write them down. Connect each of these main thoughts to the central thought using a line.

Step 3: Freely associate - As ideas emerge, write down one or two word descriptions of the ideas on lines branching from the central focus or main thougths. Allow the ideas to expand outward into branches and sub- branches. Put down all ideas without judgment or evaluation.

Step 4: Think as fast as you can - Come up with an explosion of ideas. Translate them in words, images, codes or symbols. Do what ever works for you. This is your mind map and it has to reflect the way you think.

Step 5: There are no boundaries - Think "outside-of the-box". Everything is possible. Use wild colours, fat coloured markers, crayons, or skinny felt tipped pens.

Step 6: Don´t judge your thoughts - Remember, Everything is possible. What seems to be unrelated may be relevant later. Think like you are brainstorming or your mind will get stuck and you'll never generate those great ideas.

Step 7: Don't stop to think - If ideas slow down, draw empty lines, and watch your brain automatically find ideas to put on them. If you are using different colours, change them to reenergise your mind. Stand up and mind map on a whiteboard to generate even more energy.

Step 8: Add relationships and connections - Sometimes you will see relationships and connections immediately and you can add sub-branches to a main idea. Sometimes you don't, so you just connect the ideas to the central thought. Organisation can always come later; the first requirement is to get the ideas out of your head and onto the paper. .

In mind mapping, the information in your head is arranged in a way that actually resembles how your brain works. Aside from it helping you become analytical, it also gives you the chance to be artistic. Imagine the shapes, words, and colors and how you interconnect all of them. That certainly takes more than plain ability to write, right?

Now, how do you exactly draw a mind map?

First off, it would be better to use landscape orientation on your paper so you can have a wider space to work on. Start in the middle part of the blank page. Draw or write the idea you wish to develop. Then, create subtopics for your main one. Connect all the subtopics to the center by using a line. Do the same procedure for your subtopics. Create lower-level subtopics whenever applicable. This is the basic structure of how to mind map.

Now, although there is a basic structure on what a mind map must be like, there really is no strict regulation on how you should create it. Meaning, visually, you are free to create it however you like. For instance, you can use different drawings, symbols, shapes, and colors. The more visual you are in mind mapping, the better. You don't have to be an "artist" to make your own map. Just do it the way you think best.

Ideally, the topics on your mind map must be short. If you can, simply use pictures. It is often very tempting to write long phrases when you are taking down notes to make sure that you won't forget your thoughts. However, in mind mapping, this is not advisable. The more concise you are when you mind map, the better. It will make your map more effective.

The text you use would also be important. You must change their sizes, colors, and alignments. Create visual cues in order to emphasize important details. This will make it easier for you to find what you would be looking for in the future. Remember that every little variation in your mind map engages your brain.

Mind mapping is truly useful and the nice thing about creating it is it's absolutely fun. There are plenty of places to learn how to mind map and you can easily access them online. However, do not feel compelled to follow any specific guideline. You should never worry about doing your mind map the "right way" because there really is no stringent rule in making one. The important thing is you follow its main structure. Then, enjoy the process of doing it!

So now you have a mind map. It may look like a mess but if you have followed the 8 steps you should have a very clear picture of the thoughts you have mapped. Take a second look and see how your thoughts now have flow and clarity. How you use your mind maps is really up to you but now you have a way to thinking in a much clearer and effective manner

## Chapter 8: How To Use A Mind Map

When you are trying to solve a problem, one of the toughest challenges is to move away from standards and stand-by thinking to use your imagination and think creatively to come up with the solution. Mind mapping allows you to do that.

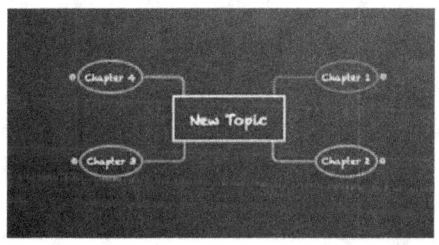

When you create your mind map for a problem, you place the problem in the center and then brainstorm ideas around it. Start by titling the branches out from the center with unusual options that will help you think in a different direction. Try "Textures", "Animals", "Shapes", "People", "Transportation" and so on. Then when you branch out from these lines, you might think like this:

Animals - How would a beaver figure this out? Obviously a beaver is not going to put on a suit and tie and walk into your office and solve your software problem, but a beaver is a builder, right, so you can begin to think on those lines.

Textures - What if we made this out of Burberry carpeting? Or slimly yummy grape jelly? Again, you are not actually going to construct an office chair out of grape jelly - even for Lady Gaga, but the idea is to get you thinking in very "way off-the-beaten-path" terms.

Many individuals who come across mind mapping wonder if it is for them. They may say they have no artistic ability or that mind mapping looks complicated and seems hard to learn. There are probably several other excuses for someone not to engage in mind mapping, but there are equally as many, if not more, benefits for learning and using mind mapping at work, school and home.

A mind map is so named because is literally allows you to "map" out your ideas and thoughts, using connections, triggers and associations to encourage and inspire other ideas. Mind maps extract the ideas from your head to create something structured and visible.

Research into the workings of the brain has shown that it operates best on a foundation of association and will link every piece of information, memory and idea to thousands and thousands of concepts. When you construct a mind map, it is extremely similar to the circular rather than liner functions of the brain, that you will be able to learn, memorize, organize and problem-solve much faster and easier than with a simple list style tool.

Problem Solving - Constructing a mind map allows you to think with countless clarity on a problem you are trying to solve. It helps you explore relationships between elements and ideas of an argument to generate one or more solutions. Since you are not tied to a "ridged structure" with linear thinking, you will find it easier to incorporate and organize new information plausibly. Mind mapping puts a new outlook on a problem so you can see the significant questions and explore choices on the stage of the big picture.

Creativity - Mind maps are an excellent tool for inspiring creativity and allowing you to produce new ideas through brainstorming. Also, the spatial layout of the mind map will assist you in gaining a better indication of the "big picture" and make connections in a more visible way. This allows for the design of an unlimited number of links, ideas, associations and thoughts on each topic put through the mind map method.

Planning and Organizing - Mind mapping is an enormously useful tool to use before beginning a project. Mind mapping will help you plan and organize your thoughts, ideas and the information into "compartmentalized" and visual bite-size pieces to help you avoid becoming stuck somewhere along the way during the execution of the task.

Memory - Using mind mapping has shown to drastically improve recall of all types of information and data over the use of conventional note taking or list making. Mind mappings unique combination of colors, spatial-visual arrangement and color lends itself to working in a way the brain enjoys and therefore allows memory to come naturally.

Learning - When used in a classroom setting, mind mapping has shown to bring a sense of renewed passion and interest from students. Mind mapping helps to instill a sense of mastery at a new skill when used for various assignments.

Teaching - Because mind mapping is a flexible tool, it lends itself to usage in several different types of academic purposes. Due to the visual cues in mind mapping, using them in the classroom offers an operational tactic for encouraging better understanding by students.

Collaborations - Use mind maps for working together with others to develop or improve plans, implement projects and share information on a large-scale. Mind mapping allows the connecting of each member's input in a creative and dynamic way.

## Chapter 9: Building Mind Maps The Right Way

Brainstorming and mind mapping are not the same and are not an interchangeable concept, but they could be used together to obtain common goals such as problem-solving, focusing research, and developing the structure for a project or any large chunk of information.

First, mind mapping is thinking, planning, and a note-taking tool that can be used in many different contexts, not only with brainstorming. Next, brainstorming can be conducted with many different office products such as Post-it notes, flip-charts, 3×5 index cards, or mind maps.

Brainstorming—it is intended to expand your thinking on a particular topic or subject and is often done in groups or meetings and as part of a team or as an exercise to build upon one another's ideas.

Mind mapping—mind mapping can then be used to organize the outcome of the brainstorming session and help realize the relationships between ideas and different content.

The two-stage process consists of stage one (free thinking) and stage two (organizing stage). These two stages should be done in this order and never mixed together for best results.

Stage One

Brainstorming = Free Thinking + Producing Ideas

Using a blank piece of paper, write your problem or topic in the center.

Start with colored pencils and markers and free association. Write and draw anywhere on the paper about anything that comes to mind regarding or related to the topic in the center. Do not edit or filter yourself or go back and cross out or erase anything on the paper, just allow your thoughts and ideas to flow, no matter how bad or outrageous you think they might be.

Stage Two

Mind Mapping = Identifying Relationships + Organizing Ideas

Using words, arrows, and lines in various colors, identify and link the relationship between the key points and ideas on your brainstorming paper to create a mind map.

When you have completed the second step, you can begin to look at your mind map to find similarities and contrasts and cause and effect to help you solve a problem, focus your research or organize the ideas and notes you've just mapped out.

Mind Mapping, the Analogy Method

The analogy method is basically shifting ideas, concepts, and thoughts from other areas to help locate a solution to a problem.

1. On a sheet of paper, formulate two branches that will serve as the main areas. Label one "Ideas" and the other "Concept Area."

2. Under the Concept Area, add a sub-branch with a larger space for topics you are reasonably knowledgeable in. These topics could be anything from "knot tying" or "toy shipbuilding" to "accounting." The topics do not have to be related to the field or profession of your problem.

3. For each of the topic areas chosen in step 2, list several major concepts relating to that area. For the knot tying area, you might write "figure of eight," "overhand knot," "double fisherman's knot," "Strangle knot," and so on.

4. It is now time to relocate ideas from step 3 to your problem. If your problem was an issue with creating costumes for a play, you could use some of the knot-tying lists to come up with creative ideas to solve the issue. For example, if one set of costumes needed to be switched on-stage

from a man's suit to a woman's long skirt; you might find the solution in the "Overhand knot."

# Chapter 10: Studying And Note Taking With Mind Maps

Mind maps are excellent tools to help you with your studying and also with note taking from seminars, meetings or from books. Because they engage your whole brain and unleash your creativity, they help you to remember and organize facts and data. You can literally recall vast amounts of information just from looking at your mind map.

When creating a mind map for studying and note taking you need to really have multiple mind maps (or layers in a software program) for the subject. A single mind map would take up a very large piece of paper.

If you start with a single sheet of paper and have the main subject in the middle and then draw your mind map out for the top level subjects and notes. Then you create additional mind maps on separate pieces of paper for each topic within the main subject. If you are using software to create your mind map then you can layer your mind maps in some of the tools provided, otherwise just linking together pieces of paper can work.

Some people though prefer to buy a large sheet of paper and create one big mind map. Whether you choose this or separate pieces of paper is entirely up to you and depends on what you feel more comfortable with.

If you are using a mind map to take notes then you may want to create a mind map for each chapter of a book, for example, and then a higher-level mind map to encompass all of the concepts and information within the book.

Mind-mapping for studying and note taking is done in the same way as a normal mind map, except you may want to include a little bit more information on it. You don't want to write out lots and lots of info on your mind map but you do want enough for you to recall the information whilst taking care not to add so much that you get overwhelmed.

So if you were mind-mapping to take notes on the Olympics you may produce something like this:

You can see that the main topic is in the middle and then there are the 'chapter' headings surrounding this and then more detail on each one.

The key here is that each of the points captures something in a few words. When you read "New Stadium Built" above it reminds you of the Olympic complex that was built and you can have other facts about this too.

"Held In East London" triggers other information, like it was held in Stratford in East London and then it follows on with more information.

Some people prefer to write out notes by hand and then draw a mind map from the notes. They can then refer to the notes as well as the mind map.

Using a mind map is a great aid to studying and you will find that it helps you to encapsulate information very concisely. By glancing at your mind map you can very quickly recall large amounts of information because the mind map triggers the release of information in your brain.

Using pictures rather than words can be extremely effective when using a mind map to help you study. Most people who use mind maps whilst studying, report that they find it easier to mentally organize and recall information plus they are less stressed about their studying. 'Mind mappers' find their exams are easier because they can easily recall the information and can relate the facts to each other, allowing them to answer questions well.

## Chapter 11: How To Design A Mind Map—Obstacles And Challenges

As previously noted, a mind map is a diagram that can be made or used to outline information in a visual manner. It is a format for linking concepts together in order to solve a problem or see the big picture. In designing a mind map for overcoming your obstacles and meeting your challenges, you will want to define the central issue and link it to another concept and link that to more detailed concepts and continue drilling it down until you find your solution. So let's get started. Let's say you are using the mind map technique to run a board meeting and you are working with your team of directors. First of all, let your team know what the process will help them do such as:

· Visualize their brainstorming, their ideas and their concepts.
· Help turn their brainstorming into

definitive action plans.
· Hold more effective and productive meetings.
· Create all your project management tools/Gantt charts, timelines, and work structures.
· Create all your project management reports, RFP's, outlines, and plans.
· Create work schedules for each member of the project team.

With these goals in mind for your mind mapping session, fill in your team on the basic ideas associated with mind mapping. Help them to understand the basics before you start. Share with them these features of mind mapping:

· Your main idea, concept or challenge expressed as a visual image (or word image).
· Themes will flow out from this central vision and these are known as branches.
· The branches have key words/images associated with them.
· Twigs will come off your branches and these will be less relevant than the key

vision and the branches themselves.
· A nodal structure is formed by the branches.

Once your team understands these concepts then you can walk through the actual design of a mind map. You can do this in ten steps. Let's review the steps then we will look at an actual mind map using what we have learned here:

1. List your core concept or challenge. This should be one word and place it in the middle of your empty piece of paper. This can be a word or an image, whichever your team is most comfortable with.
2. Out of this core image should flow your main branches. These are ideas/themes/images that your team develops from your core image.

(Example if your core image was Agenda – as in our prior example- then your branches might be Opening, New Business, Financial Reports, Fundraising Plans, Old Business, and Closing)
3. Then you would have the smaller lines

or twigs that came off of each branch such as for the Fundraising branch, your team might brainstorm all the things that needed to be done to make your fundraiser a success. This might include catering, open bar, marketing, ticket sales, advertising, program, public relations, volunteers, venue selection, set up, break down and so on. Each one of these is a twig coming off the Fundraising line.
4. Keep going until you run out of ideas—be creative in your drawing. You are not making a diagram. You are using your entire brain, not just your analytical part of it.
5. Revise your mind map as needed until the entire team is satisfied with it. Remember, you can revise it or insert new information at any time. You do not have to redo it if you decide to change one branch or twig.

http://www.mindmappingexamples.com

Thoughts to keep in mind as your team develops this and other mind maps:

· Practice makes perfect. You will get more and more creative as you make more mind maps and play with the techniques more.
· Use images as well as words. This is very powerful and acts to free up your creative thought process.
· Use colored pencils, markers, or chalk so that your mind map is dynamic and inviting to look at.
· Be sure that your thought process starts from the middle and radiates out to the branches and twigs.
· Try to avoid phrases or sentences and stick with a keyword like you would if you were building a website.
· Don't be intimidated—move quickly and uses symbols and images as much as possible. If you need to reference outside sources, use different colors to do so.
· Use capital letters and print to make it easier to conceptualize at a glance. Make your branches and twigs the same length as your word or images, symbols and codes.
· Keep your branches connected to your central concept and your twigs connected

to your branches. The further from the center a line is the smaller and lighter in color it should be. The further from the center concept a symbol, code, image, or keyword is the less relevant it is.

Keeping all of this in mind, try to practice this type of mind map on your own or with a group of friends, peers or group.

## Chapter 12: General Benefits

This section plots the right method to make a psyche map. There are numerous various approaches to make mind maps and a wide range of approaches to utilize them. Indeed, a plenty of various principles have been built up for assembling them. Brain maps don't need to be done likewise way each and every time. They are adaptable commonly. In any case, there are a few things that you should do so as to get the most incentive out of them.

At the point when you are making a brain map, it is ideal to utilize solitary watchwords. This implies you need to utilize particular ideas and solitary thoughts, rather than attempting to fit various thoughts into one point or subtopic. You need to break these thoughts or pieces into the littlest structure conceivable so that your subtopics can neatly sever of that one theme with no disarray. You are truly following one single idea, information point, or thought.

At the point when you make a principle subject, it ought to so completely epitomize that primary thought so that the supporting subtopics effectively identify with the fundamental watchword. For instance, by and large you wouldn't have any desire to utilize something like 'Natural products and Vegetables' for your principle watchword. Rather, you would need to utilize the catchphrase 'Foods grown from the ground' with subtopics like 'Banana', 'Apple', 'Orange', and so on. That permits you to take a gander at that particular primary subject of leafy foods comprehend all that is related with that principle subject of 'Natural product'. For this situation, all that follows ought to be a sort of natural product.

Normally when you see subtopics falling off of a subject, the relationship is one to where the fundamental thought continues. There is transaction of the thought, or fundamental idea, descending. Thus, with the fundamental subject being 'Leafy foods' being a subtopic, you realize that 'Apple' is a kind of natural product. It is that unmistakable connection that gives the progressive system that was made so much force. That is the reason you follow solitary catchphrases.

Presently, a less explicit approach to consider this is the length of the branch ought to be equivalent to the word. Subtopics ought not be sections and passages of substance. At most it ought to be a short sentence, comprised of only a couple of words. Something very similar applies to primary subjects and the focal point. You don't need a goliath mind map that is stacked with words. You need to be as compact as could reasonably be expected. This length necessity isn't generally a prerequisite by any means, only a rule that ought to be followed.

Principle theme lines can be thicker than subtopic lines. This emblematically shows the primary subjects are all the more impressive or all the more firmly identified with the focal point.

This visual portrayal gives you a ton of data initially. A similar rule applies to bolts. Incidentally, if there are bolts utilized, this emblematically expresses 'it's of this sort', 'it's identified with', or 'the data streams toward that path'. Along these lines, at times you will see bolts in a brain map, and now and then you won't on the grounds that bolts allude to the data stream.

The last rule is that you should gather like things. You can do this in an assortment of ways. You can utilize comparative shapes or comparable hues to aggregate data. Simply the way that you have a focal subject prompting a primary point which thusly leads into subtopics says something. You are stating that this data is connected, which is basically the general purpose of collection in a brain map.

How the data is introduced outwardly reveals to you a horrendous part, even initially. You can move these points and subtopics around whenever to reexamine or rearrange these subjects varying to show that one 'holds more weight' than another, etc. This is particularly simple to do when utilizing programming.

These rules were intended to assist you with understanding the essential guidelines for making mind maps and the purposes behind each. Obviously, you can defy these guidelines whenever. You can arrange the data in any capacity that causes you best. Be that as it may, realizing these standards can assist you with conveying to yourself as well as other people all the more adequately.

# Chapter 13: Benefits Of Using A Mind Map

General Benefits

There are countless reasons to consider making a mind map, but for the sake of ease, consider the ten benefits we have listed for you below. Chances are that one of them will hit home with you!

1. They take up less space than chronologically based notes and are simple and effective to produce and use later

Often, we can take pages and pages of notes. In effort to catch the most important ideas, we write everything down. It's fine to do that the first time around (if you need to), but then take the truly important information from your 20 pages of notes, and consolidate them into one.

2. Mind mapping encourages organized thinking.

Our thoughts come quickly and they aren't always connected for us. Writing them as they come to mind will allow you to group like aspects. Also, having everything on one page eliminates the need to search for documents and information. Imagine what you can do with all of the time saved searching for missing papers!

3. Mind mapping can be used in any situation.

Perhaps the greatest advantage of mind mapping is that you can use it regardless of the situation you are in. For example, you can use mind maps to reorganize your personal life, to change your daily habits, or to facilitate the professional development process.

4. Mind mapping helps you make better decisions.

The process of mind mapping is based on the human brain's ability to store an unlimited number of connections and schemas. When you have more information stored in your long term memory, you will begin to make much more effective choices.

5. Mind maps provide for more effective studying

Because everything is laid out before you on one piece of paper, your brain has a greater chance of making connection between materials. These connections are called anchors. Giving your brain as many anchors as possible when trying to retrieve information is critical. You already have many anchors and may not even realize it. How often have you walked into a store only to have been confronted by a smell? That smell has the capability of taking you right back to your grandmother's perfume when you were eight years old (or whatever your specific anchor may be). The same is true for mind maps. The color, shapes, size, and so on are anchors for your brain. (This will be covered in greater detail in 6.4.2)

## 6. Mind maps are an efficient means of record keeping and reflection

An obvious way they would serve as record keeping is in using them in a journal/diary capacity, but this doesn't necessarily need to be the case. If you make a mind map at the start of every day to plan your day, and then tuck those mind maps into a drawer, you will be able to refer back to the set every 20-30 days (or whatever number you like) to measure your progress. Are you giving yourself unrealistic amounts of work each day? Perhaps you aren't challenging yourself enough. Where are you focusing too much of your time? In this instance, the mind maps will serve as a snapshot of your productivity without having to riffle through pages of agenda notes.

## 7. Mind mapping will strengthen your memory

As we get older, our ability to retain information for long periods of time begins to diminish. Research shows that this breakdown of ability can be reversed with proper training. Because of all of the anchors provided, your brain is working to retrieve information from storage with greater ease. Over time, you will find that you are remembering greater details with minimal effort.

8. Mind maps clear your mind to increase productivity

Productivity experts suggest that getting all of your thoughts down on paper will allow you to be more productive. If you are spending your time thinking about what needs to be done, you aren't taking action. Author of Getting Things Done, David Allen, suggests that it's more than making a to-do list. A to-do list is still a list of unfinished tasks that you are left to think about with no real plan devised. Mind maps are the solution to this. You are able to push each task out further into steps so that you are actively considering how to achieve them. This will allow you to focus solely on one task at a time.

9. Mind maps help you keep a well-oiled home

Busy parents and children rarely have time to check calendars, so having a central mind map can be a solution to knowing where everybody is at a glance. In addition to schedules, mind maps can be made to achieve financial goals, plan parties, organize grocery trips, and more! We'll cover the extensive list of benefits for a family in chapter 6.

10. Mind maps are a lot of fun to make!

You have far more control over the creativity that takes place while creating a mind map as opposed to a linear list. No matter whether you are creating a map on the computer or with markers and paper, the creation of one should be a fun process for you!

Though this was just a quick overview, I hope that you are already thinking of the possibilities in your life. As you continue reading, you will find detailed and specific examples of their use for every aspect of your life.

On a larger scale, mind mapping is highly beneficial for groups and organizations as well. The beauty of this technique is that it can be adapted according to every person or organization's unique and individual needs. Mind mapping can help you to unlock your creativity so that you don't forget important details.

Once you begin making mind maps to organize your thoughts and ideas, you will start to see how useful they can be.

## Chapter 14: Why Mind Mapping?

Because the mind jumps from one thing to another, and not in an orderly fashion, linear thinking is extremely limiting. Mind mapping helps you avoid linearly thought processes. A mind map can open your way of thinking in a new and creative direction. Some might say "outside the box." Mind maps are more realistic than lists because like nearly all of life, they are not orderly and ridged, to begin with.

As you tap into your right brain hemisphere, where intuition and creativity can be of use, mind mapping encourages problem-solving in ways you would not have thought of when using lists and your left, analytical hemisphere of the brain alone. Problems and difficulties are not always going to fit neatly into an outline type arrangement.

Let's say you have ten things you need to get done today. You take out a slip of lined paper, and you list them under the heading "To Do Today," so you will not forget what to do before you crawl into bed tonight. This is what your list looks like when you're done:

To Do Today

- Gas up truck.

- Lunch with Tony.

- Email manager.

- Grocery store for birthday party food.

- Finish PowerPoint presentation for Thursday.

- Gym—spinning class.

- Pay bills today—online.

- Help Susie with the science project.

- Call client for next meeting date/time.

- Give Spot a bath.

The items on your "To Do Today" list are recorded linearly in a neat numerical and plain layout. Basically, everything you need to complete today is written down; however, there are no colors, pictures, or other images to create a more visually stimulating and interesting list.

Using the mind mapping technique, lay out your same "To-Do Today" list in a sprawling style with more space between each item. Then each of the things that need to be done is separated between work and home (or personal and professional if you like). Adding color to the text and connector lines help to engage your right brain hemisphere and so will adding pictures and images.

An example of a mind mapping "To-Do Today" style list would have color and pictures to make the list fun and more memorable. For instance, the task "Give Spot a bath" could have a drawing of your dog Spot next to a bathtub following the line that reads "Give Spot a bath." The qualities of the mind map are more dimensional, vivid images, and colors help enhance each of the components.

The idea behind a making a to-do list is to have a reminder for the tasks you must complete in a given time frame, in this case, a single day. The written list is problematic from the start for several reasons. For one thing, its construction does not enable easy memorization; it forces review of the list several times during the day. This can also be challenging as it is a time-waster hunting for the list, even if your list is on an electronic device. And if you lose the list, you cannot refer to it, and its construction is not meant for your memory; therefore, you will most likely forget several of the items needed to be done on your list.

Mind mapping will allow you to create your "To Do Today" list and still use a check-mark system that many individuals find gives them a feeling of accomplishment. Small boxes for checking off "done" tasks can be placed next to each line item if you wish, and after all, the mind map is your creation, and you can fashion it any way that works for you.

# Chapter 15: How To Teach Your Children Mind Mapping

Would you like to make reading more fun for your children while studying? Do you want to help them ace their school tests? If so, there are amazing things you can teach your child from this book. Most people are already aware of mind mapping. Have you started using it already? The main reason why it is so effective is that it utilizes both sides of your brain. It uses the more analytical left side in forming words and relationships, and the more colorful or creative right side in forming images and colors. This does wonders for adults: Normally, we tend to use our left side of the brain more often, using more words as opposed to images, and more relationships as opposed to colors. On the other hand, children tend to work the other way round. Young children who are not conversant with the adult way of thinking find drawing pictures natural;

you can take advantage of this and teach them mind mapping.

The moment your children learn how to use mind mapping technique, they will have an edge over other children who are not using the same tools. They will be able to outline stories and ideas much more easily, create better notes, and summarize books more quickly. In other words, they find it much more fun to be in school. They will enjoy studying, and subsequently get better grades.

However, keep in mind that you are not a teacher, but rather a coach. Your work is to show your child different ways to outline books, thoughts, and ideas, so do not judge, and do not impose ideas.

First, ensure that your child has a couple of different pens and a big sheet of paper. Your only work is to tell your child that the following exercise is something they need to draw; they can be as creative as they want.

Tell a story or pick something from one of their school books, ensuring that you use sufficient image words, i.e. words that can be easily transformed into images. While reading from the book or telling your story, allow your child to draw. Once you are through, and your child has drawn the pictures, ask them to repeat the story using their drawing. Can they manage? Is their story pretty much the same as the one you narrated? If so, both of you did a marvelous job. If not, what led to the discrepancy? Were the pictures not as powerful, or did you possibly use inefficient image words? Investigate together.

When your child manages to do this, you can go a step further if you want. Get a new sheet of paper and segregate it into a couple of areas, according to the number of topics in your story. Start the process all over again. Your child draws as you talk. Just ensure that you draw each topic in its own section. Then ask your child to use the drawing to recall the story, and let them have a pen to draw a line connecting one part of the story to the other, which will be your branch.

If there are any other parts that could use more sub branches, ask your child to add more images with more pictures. The end result is that your child creates something that resembles a real mind map, or even better.

Furthermore, you can go an extra mile by giving your child a new sheet of paper to recreate the whole mind map from memory, after you have created the map. Of course, you can provide hints as to what to add in case they are lost.

The last step is to step away from your child, give them a book to go through, and let them create the story and images by themselves. This will help your child know how to outline their books, thoughts, ideas and a lot more using a visual map, without your help. The mind map may not be very convincing to the conventional mind mappers, but it helps them achieve their goals while enjoying themselves.

Do not fret if your child fails to create a perfect mind map. Remember it is not about perfect maps, but rather your child handling information in a more efficient and smarter manner with more fun. However, the whole process of your child being able to achieve this will depend on their interest in the topics, their age, and perhaps whether it is a wonderful weather outside.

# Chapter 16: Mind Mapping Techniques

A MIND map is a handy tool for busy people. It enables them to productively and efficiently plan, organise and present information.

A MIND map promotes broader thinking, better troubleshooting and is a valuable instrument for team cooperation.

Here are only ten ways to use a map. The maximum number of options is indefinite.

Usages.

**1. A mind map is a perfect tool to create new ideas.** The unstructured style allows a free flow of ideas and information.

Because of the clustered principles, it encourages theories to move between subjects instead of pushing them down a list.

2. Work management:

A mind map is an optimal work scheduling system. Themes usually arranged around the primary purpose of the meeting, with details from there.

The virtual chart on the screen (or discussed in an informal gathering) helps members to review topics, attach action items, set deadlines and agree. All the mental can show on the map, which is then electronically shared after the meeting ends.

3. Brainstorm Chart

While considering the different factors to be taken into account when making a significant decision, a mind map can be a helpful tool.

Listing various alternatives, advantages and disadvantages, and other considerations will build creative thinking and contribute to an informed decision.

4. The decision to create a mind map

Many busy people find that using a mental map is a great way to organise information and activities.

5. Strategic thought maps are a perfect way to plan a corporate strategy.

Mind maps may use in a variety of ways in the decisive planning phase, from straightforward SWOT analyses to decision making and the creation of specific tactics.

6. Mind diagram for the intelligence organisation

Event preparation A mind map works when collaborating on an incident involving various sponsors, visitors and a variety of organising activities.

7. Mind Map Activity Planning

Planning a project with a mental map enables tasks to be arranged from broad categories and split into smaller parts.

The change of activities makes it much easier to delegate, schedule and predict the timetable.

You can turn the SmartDraw mental map with a simple click into a Gantt chart or allocate some concept or action element to it using Trello.

**8**. Presentations In performance environments, the mind maps work exceptionally well.

Mind map diagrams are an exciting way to present information, not bullet-point lists.

For Excel, Microsoft Word and Google Docs, and more, SmartDraw mind maps are more comfortable to import.

**9**. Evaluation of situations Sometimes, difficulties arise, and evaluation is required.

For this purpose, a mind map is an excellent tool. It helps you to research and organise various aspects of the problem in related areas.

Thinking about and physically capturing such a scenario can also encourage seeking alternatives.

## 10. Taking Notes In workshops.

Classes, online programs and for general usage daily charts, mind maps can make quickly and effectively.

## Application Of Mind Map

It commonly used worldwide. It can be used in the areas of memorisation, studying and reading, etc.as illustrated below.

1. The visual design of the mental map allows users to comprehend the points of knowledge easily; to understand the relationship across lines and to see the entire picture.

2. Encourage comprehension through Mind Map Visualize concepts with fewer texts and more images to make them more visual and readable.

3. Taking note of the mind map is inspiring, elegant and expressive. It is undoubtedly a concise and clear way to save time and effort.

4. Combined with brainstorm, mind maps will help to develop thoughts to find further ideas and to compose materials.

5. Using Mind Map, A mental plan will arrange speech material and help speakers to remember the principal concepts and information better. The speaker will be able to speak more fluently in this manner.

6. Promote invention and imagination Systemic and rational reasoning can produce more creative ideas and therefore encourage innovation.

7. Firstly, this method helps people to discover challenges in time through simulation. Through a detailed analysis of concepts, mind maps can encourage people to think more closely. A comprehensive and systematic comprehension of the issue will speed it up.

8. Brain Map Self-Analysis Learning all virtues and demerits. Create plans to improve yourself.

9. Mind Map Planning provides a structured, standardised and straightforward way to schedule and visually display activities, time and location.

At the same time, the designer will easily compare all activities and assign importance.

10. Mind Map Goals.

Set short-term or long-term goals and aesthetically.

Divide objectives into different realistic targets. Allow intervention more sensible to pursue success.

11. Foster Mind Map.

Learning Teachers should show information in a well-organized way, using a mind map, so that students understand better.

The visualisation may also help include pupils, promote interest and improve memory.

Using Mind Mapping To Achieve Your Goals.

Realising one's life goals does not happen by accident but by proper planning.

Proper planning means a systemic approach to achieve what you have outlined.

One of the techniques by which you can plot your direction and reach your goal is through the use of the mind mapping technique.

**To do so,** you will first grasp what this method is and how it works.

What is mind mapping?

Mind mapping is a method made famous by Tony Buzan, a TV personality.

He made specific recommendations for how to achieve it, but everybody can freely draw up his mind map because it is all about creative thinking.

There are many examples of how a visual diagram is and how it can be easily confused with so many variations as to how it would feel.

That's why it is essential to go back to the basics.

**In essence, a mental map contains the following elements:** a central topic or main idea, subjects or ideas linked to the fundamental concept, connectors that connect the subtopics with the original design and drawings or colours, to emphasise ideas.

If you see a drawing of the neural network, the basic unit of the nervous system, the diagram of the mind appears very like this.

It has a central structure called the nucleus with everything else -the soma, dendrites, and the axon -radiating from it.

It may be the reason why the mind map is an excellent way to express one's creative thinking and keep the juice of ideas flowing.

Structurally, the mind map follows the basic unit of the human brain.

How Is Mind Mapping Used To Achieve Goals?

Based on the mind mapping technique, you can take steps to help you achieve your life goals.

Resources Needed a clean sheet of paper to mark pencils or crayons (preferably bright ones) eraser

Step 1.

Before you use the mind map as an objective, you should have a clear idea of your goal.

If you have many targets, you're going to need several blank pieces of paper for each goal. Have one goal for one mind-mapping exercise.

Two questions can ask to define the target clearly:

What do you want to do?

Is it a personal, work or career, relationship, or leisure-related goal?

Step 2.

When the ultimate target is clear in your mind, please write it down with bold strokes on a blank sheet of paper.

You may draw it in light colours to attract your eyes.

The aim should be sufficiently broad or long-term. It ensures that your target will be accomplished in a specific time frame, five to 10 years. The time frame, though, would depend a lot on the design, interest, ability and age of you.

If you want at least five books to be published, you would possibly require one year for each volume.

When you would like to write long novels that count as a bestseller, it will take five years, but it also depends on your experience or writing skill.

If you have an expected life expectancy of 70 and you are 50 years old, then you have 20 years ahead of you.

You have a lot of time to write books.

Step 3.

Talk about sub-goals or specific measures From the stated objective, talk about sub-goals or particular actions that will help you to accomplish this primary purpose.

These activities will serve as your specific objectives.

Do that freely and let your mind wander around.

Using the book example your sub-goal is as follows: describe the book's contents, download a book writing software, collect the literature that is relevant to the identified topics, write a chapter in two days, identify the publisher and submit a manuscript.

Step 4.

Reflect on your mind map. Examine your work and review what you have written down. Identify which of these goals you want to achieve first or can be made first. Write them down and plan logically.

Add a time frame for each sub-target. If necessary, break the sub-target into sub-targets to make it clear which certain things you should do gradually to achieve the primary goal.

Step 5.

Just do it. Well, if you look at your mental map, nothing happens. It is paralysis or overanalysis. Decision and do what to do. Time is gold.

## Chapter 17: Using Colors

One of the main things which separates mind maps from normal note taking (aside from the structure) is the use of colors. The creators of the mind mapping technique recommend using at least 3 colors in your mind maps and I wholeheartedly agree. One of the downsides of a mind map is that the branches can become visually confusing easily. By using colors you will be able to clearly see the different branches.

One of the ways I use colors in my mind maps is to indicate emotions. I have not seen anyone else recommending this in all my research but I have found this to be a very useful and powerful addition to the technique, I hope it is as useful for you as it has been for me.

The main idea is to color code all of the branches with the colors of the rainbow (Red, orange, yellow, green, blue, purple) and to associate each of those different colors with an emotion. This is best used to consolidate a story or as a way of journaling/ brainstorming since most of the time business and college notes are not very emotionally stimulating. The main way I use this technique is to summarize topics which I really care about, the most recent of which was a seminar I watched about how to start an importing business from china. After taking notes on the seminar I sat down and drew a new mind map but coded it based on my emotions about the various aspects of the business. For example if something about the business made me sad then it would be blue.

Another great way to use this technique is to get various colors of highlighters and then to highlight a black and white mind map with your emotions. This looks visually chaotic but it can serve to turn an organized mind map of ideas into an emotionally rich tapestry which will be easier and more fun to remember.

Here are the associations I use for the colors of the rainbow, you can feel free to modify or change these as you like but this is what works for me (and what most artists and interior designers consider the associations of the colors)

Red

Aggression, passion, drive, stamina- red is an energizing color, it is full of fire and passion, and whenever I feel aggression or any very intense and high valence emotion I highlight it in red. Often times these things are not just what you feel passionately for, but also ideas which you are adamantly against!

Orange

Pleasure, optimism, expression – When I use orange it is to indicate ideas or points which make me feel optimistic and points which I would want to share, these ideas are ideas that make your heart skip a beat and make you get excited for the future, potentially world changing discoveries, a new relationship, an idea which you know will change your life for the better, etc...

Yellow

Fun, creativity, logic – I rarely use yellow in my notes but when I do it is normally to signal ideas which are creative. If I am reading a book for a class and I find some of the ideas to be unique and creative, things I would never think to use then I will highlight them in yellow to show this. Often times I use yellow to highlight points which just seem to come from a different point of view than mine.

Green

Balance, calm, nature, connection – Green has a feeling of harmony and natural-ness to me so I use it to add emotion to particularly clear or well thought out ideas, or any ideas which make me feel calm. Another great use of the color green is to indicate harmony, if you are taking notes on a fiction book for example, green might be used whenever a character is acting in a congruent manner which seems honest. Or if you are taking notes on philosophy green might mean an idea which is harmonious with your nature and resonates with what you feel to be true.

Blue

Peace, emotional depth, sadness – Blue is a color which is very emotionally deep, often times it is symbolic of sadness and because of this I use it when I hear things which give me that icy feeling of falling in my chest. Often times blue can be used for calm as well but I find that for me it seems to have more impact as an indicator of sadness

Purple

Intuition, imagination, meditation, the color of royalty – I use purple to symbolize the sublime, the more spiritual and subtle emotions which are aroused in me when reading or listening to a lecture.

Hopefully you find these color guides useful, it is important to remember that these colors have nothing to do with what the content you are taking notes on is but only with your subjective experience of the content. In order for this technique to be at all useful for you you have to come back in touch with the way you feel about ideas and then be able to clearly identify the feeling and what causes it. This technique will not be for everyone but for those who relate it will be invaluable.

Using Indicators[v][vi]

The techniques in this chapter were inspired by another note taking system known as the bullet journal. The bullet journal is an analog note taking. system that lets you organize the past present and future.

Using the techniques of bullet journaling with your mind maps will be useful to add more information into your confined space

The bullet journal is a note taking system to keep track of the things which you have to do but there is an interesting idea which we can incorporate into our mind maps to make them more effective

The idea which we are going to incorporate is called "Signifiers" Signifiers are little symbols like an asterisk an exclamation point, a smiley face, etc. and we standardize them across all of our notes so that whenever we are looking for a certain type of idea all we need to do is spot the signifiers. For example, you might have a signifier for good quotes, ideas which will be on a test, inspirational thoughts, discussion points, etc... and as you get better and better acquainted with using them you will be able to spot more opportunities to use them.

If you are using a journal for all of your mind maps it is a good idea to place the indicators in the back like a key on a map. Then you can go back to them periodically and check to make sure that you are still using them consistently. This little idea is one of my favorite ways to boost the power of mind maps because it will let you find information rapidly

Here is a useful list of indicators:

☐- idea you like

☐ idea that makes you sad

*point to remember

! Clever point

!! Brilliant point

? Discussion subject

?? Something you disagree with

% Statistic to remember

"..." Quote written down on the back of the page

Thought bubble – original ideas to be added

Feel free to expand on this little list of signifiers and add them on the opposite side of the line than the word you wrote down. Using signifiers often will drastically increase how useful your notes become for review session because you will have instant access to any type of idea you want.

When you should and should not use mind maps

Mind maps are amazing tools an 9 times out of 10 they are a better alternative to traditional note taking but like any tool there is a time and a place to use it and a time and a place not to. Mind maps are great for connecting diverse ideasm and to keep track of ideas which don't come in sequence. Mind maps are also excellent for keeping track of ideas which don't need to be captured in full sentences and ideas which don't come too fast.

The main weakness of mind maps is that they don't work for capturing full sentences and that they are a little bit slower here are the main times to go back to normal note taking

If you are in a fast paced lecture

If you have a fast paced lecturer in college or as part of your continuing education in business then mind mapping can become a real nightmare. Some people just seem to love blazing through speeches and inundating you with more information than you know what to do with. When these people speak so fast the real problem is that you don't have enough time to think about how to organize the information... because you are too busy trying to capture all of it!!

I remember one theatre teacher I used to have and she had a nasty habit of giving her lectures as a bullet point list of vital ideas which she would read as fast as humanly possible (or so it seemed) everyone in the class spent the full 60 minutes staring at their notebook feverishly writing notes and hoping to keep up. It was not uncommon that I and the people next to me would use 3-4 pages to take notes over the hour.

The best solution to situations like this is to take your notes like normal and later on at home, transform these notes into a clear mind map. Usually this will only take

30 minutes or so but you will be left with the meat of the talk you were at and the mind map will be far more useful that the confused jumble of notes that you had to chaotically scramble together in the moment.

The lecture is mainly large terms or quotes

Many times if you are attending a lecture about a topic which you are not familiar with you will find that there are dozens of terms, place names, item names, event names, etc... which you need to write down with a definition. There is nothing wrong with this but when a lecture has too many of these terms a mind map stops making sense. Earlier on we talked about how you could cite quotes on a separate piece of paper, but when the lecture is more than about 25% terminology then normal linear notes make more sense.

4 Great uses for mind maps

Life Planning

One of the best uses for mind mapping is planning out the different areas of your life and how you would like them to look like. I have had massive success at improving my vision of my future using mind mapping. Because of the generative and creative way that mind mapping works I came up with more ways to improve my life than ever before just by sitting down and doing this simple life exercise. If you haven't ever sat down to think about your life before I highly recommend you go through the following exercise to get a feeling for the power of using mind mapping to think about your own ambitions.

Step one, get your favorite software or notebook open

Step two draw yourself in the middle of the mind map.

Step three On the first level, draw out all the areas of your life which you can improve on, really try to generate as many ideas as you are able to: physical health, mental health, finances, friendships, love relationships, travel,etc...

Step four: Brainstorm what success means to you in each of these areas, what is your ideal body, your ideal relationship, etc...

Step five: once you have a web of what it is that your ideals are, brainstorm all of the things which you could possibly do to achieve your goal.

Step six, going back over your whole map, put a star next to each of the ideas or means of getting your goal which you are going to use.

Step seven: review your mind map often, even every day.

Book outlines

One of the best uses of mind mapping is to outline books and really get to the heart of the book as fast as possible. The fact that books are broken down into chapters makes outlining them on your mind map very, very easy.

Step one: Skim through the book, reading the first paragraph or page of each chapter and decide which of the chapters you are going to read. Most books have about 5 good, useful chapters and the rest is largely fluff or the same thing again and again.

Step two: Draw the book in the middle of your mind map with one branch for each of the chapters which you are going to take the time to read.

Step three: go through the chapters you chose reading the first sentence or so of each paragraph until you hit on a really good idea, once that happens, read all the way through the idea and add it to the appropriate branch of your mind map.

Step four: Review your mind map and make sure that all of the major ideas are covered and that there is nothing that you don't understand

This style of speed reading a book might seem a little unusual at first and you might even feel like you are missing out on the parts of the book which you didn't read. The truth is that reading a book cover to cover is just a convention we all follow, it isn't a rule, and by reading only the most important parts of the book you are actually able to retain more important information and you are able to understand a book better in less time than other people.

Lectures

We have already talked plenty about how to use mind maps to take notes on lectures but one funny and interesting point still has to be made. Drawing a caricature of your lecturer in the middle of your mind map really seems to help! As goofy as this is, a really well done caricature helps more than just about any other image for me (and maybe it will for you too!)

Brainstorming solutions to problems

Using mind maps to find solutions to problems you are facing is one of the best ways to overcome problems which seem insurmountable. By using a mind map you are going to be able to break a problem down into its component parts and then reconstruct it in an empowering which allows you to find the solution quickly and easily.

Step one: Write down the problem you are facing in the middle of the mind map

Step two: write out reasons that this is a problem, some of the negative effects of it as the first level of the map.

Step Three: write out potential ways to solve these symptoms of the problem on the next branches of the mind map

Step four: read all of the ways you can improve the symptoms of the problem and ask yourself "Is there some way that I can improve all of these different symptoms at once?"

You will be amazed at how often gaining a little bit of altitude on the problem and thinking about the separate aspects can be useful to synthesize a solution.

# Chapter 18: Unleash Your Imagination With Mind Mapping

Mind mapping is a great and underutilised complete brain system for solving issues, deciding, developing plans, speeding up learning and communicating effectively with others.

It is faster, fun and covers more basics than traditional methods of outlining.

Mind maps are recognised widely by British educator and brain expert Tony Buzan. His contribution to mind mapping is an innovative method that integrates keywords, visual images and icons in a free flow' tree.

' The associated key points that form the' tree' are trunks, branches and leaves. "The process ends with a logical element of analysis and alignment.

Nancy Margulies (author and artist of conceptual design) and Michael Gelb (author of "How to Think Like Leonardo da Vinci") are also practitioners in mind mapping.

The main principles and techniques of visual imaging are focused on functional psychology.

The machine penetrates the visual cortex and makes up a large proportion of the neurons of the brain. Mind mapping incorporates the intuition of the subconscious, natural curiosity and rational forces of thought.

Many participants are amazed at how easily the program catches thoughts, encourages imagination and offers practical and realistic solutions.

Despite what you might think, mental mapping requires no artistic skills.

Anybody can wander about the diagram. The primary requirement is the willingness to use the following practical and straightforward neuroscience methodology.

**Materials.**

The beginning of a large piece of paper is the perfect flip chart page.

Use colourful styles or pencils.

Buy colourful stickers with patterns, pictures and symbols that are appealing to you and relevant to the subject.

You will have creative attributes on your mind map without having artistic skill.

Methods 1.

Begin in the middle:

draw a circle or oval in the centre of the page with the topic or key concept.

A mark, illustration or acronym can apply. Even a small picture works well.

2. Use keywords:

Single representative words are preferable over phases and short phrases.

At first, it could take a little patience and practice. The growth of the ability to think in terms pays dividends since they are abundant with meaning, easy to remember and other phrases.

The associated vital words ' strings will finally describe the context of a situation and the paths to insights, solutions and desired results.

These words are potent catalysts for creative as well as rational thought. A competence worth cultivating is the effective use of keywords.

**a.** Print your most powerful concept words on the lines (to form the "tree stumps") in the middle of the page from your subject.

As an example, you can start with terms like PURPOSE, CUSTOMERS, CONCERNS, and GOALS if you want to chart your market.

Make sure you only use one word per section.

Use light, pictures and symbols.

It can be a helpful aid for your stickers. Stick characters and other understandable, hand-drawn symbols are working well.

**b.** Your words will stimulate different keywords that aligned with central ideas.

For example, CONCERNS may lead to new concepts such as FINANCING, COMPETITION and LICENSING, which can become newlines (e.g. "branches") from the CONCERNs line.

These terms of the definition would create a new sequence of words describing new lines (for example, "leaves").

Again, always use colour and images to show your words and add meaning to them. It's best to print your most important words.

3. Let it flow and go:

The operational terms when mapping the minds of this early creative stage are spontaneity, imagination and "big picture thinking."

Move as fast as you can to finish your page. Go wherever you want.

It isn't an appropriate and linear place or time.

If you have "writer's block" with any related word list, switch to another phrase, the "trunk" or "branch," which catches your eye and add words.

Keep going until you believe you have more things to deal with than enough.

4. wipe off some stress.

Get rest and ease a minute before you return to assess and organise the outcomes of your creative, free-association level. It is the part of the process that incorporates linear, reflective and rational skills.

Search for similarities, trends and connections between "strains, branches and leaves.

" Align and link portions of your "forest" with additional lines, arrows, icons and phrases, to provide more context and performance.

You can also choose which pieces you think are the most important and delete those that are trivial.

5. Redraw Mind Map:

You may want to redraw your mind map and sequence the main ideas and concepts with numbers in the direction of your clock, depending on the application.

It may be suitable for communication and training or for use as daily learning and memory aid to build a company or carry out a significant project.

In short, mind mapping reveals and unleashes the genius in your visual cortex through the power and imagination of your visual thinking to plan, learn, resolve problems and communicate with others.

You have nothing to fear except to witness your brain's ability to save your life consciously.

Use Colors and Images in Mind Maps

If you want to learn Mind Maps and how we can use them in everything we do.

It is good to get a good map book with step by step methodology guides and how to use Mind Maps to improve our productivity, planning and organisational skills.

People from all walks of life increasingly use mind maps. Students use Mind Maps to learn new knowledge, to understand new concepts and to remember the information later.

Most individuals and experts use them to brainstorm ideas, to introduce themselves to consumers, and to coordinate their staff.

Everyone can use them to improve their creativity and to achieve more by being more organised every day.

Mind Maps are so standard because they are easy to use and all sides of the brain share in the learning process.

The reasonable, logical link between thinking on the left side of the brain is the usual aim of new concepts and solutions to problems.

On the right side is the imaginative, creative side, sometimes overlooked in analytical tasks to solve problems.

But its presence is equally essential to thought and imagination because it makes it possible for you to understand concepts across the head and recall more details more quickly.

The attributes of a mental map itself tend to include the right hemisphere of the brain in the process of learning because a spiritual plan is only a picture containing information.

The diagram reveals the left side of the brain while the world represented in the centre.

The usual fair way to achieve this is to link colour lines in your Map and then use coloured wires to connect each subject to the central idea after creating all of your sub-topics instead of black lines.

Use or arrange the subtopics in a different colour for each subtopic; green for financing ideas, red for potential barriers or any other scheme you would like to use.

The strength of Mind Maps can also improve by adjusting the structure or design of the Map; if you were to know critical facts and statistical information about the fisheries industry, for example, you would wish to create a chart like a boat or a fish.

You can visualise the Map in your mind, know how many subjects were and where they were, and remember the information much more quickly.

If you thought about what your own florist business could take to start, you can shape each subtopic like flora and use the different kinds of colours of flowers to connect common themes.

It would help you or anyone with you to think about the florist's central idea while coming up with ideas.

Draw on the Map, or use the clip art.

If you use Mind Maps to instruct your pupils, using pictures or diagrams to understand the concepts you are bringing before them.

By using diagrams or pictures to reflect the points you are trying to make, you can help people to fully understand the information as introduced and to make it easier to recall later.

Mind Maps can be used as useful motivational devices as well; you can demonstrate with a graph showing a 15 per cent increase in profits the list of brainstormed ideas.

# Chapter 19: Techniques Used In Mind Mapping

After reading the various applications of mind mapping, I bet you are curious to learn some techniques. Basically, mind mapping just like any reading technique that uses visualization is a method that utilizes images and diagrams to make learning effective and comprehension easier. The truth is that mind mapping is a relatively easy note-making tool that involves limited resources. Essentially, all you need is a blank unlined paper, some colored pencils and pens, your brain and your imagination! When you start using mind mapping, you will quickly figure out that life can be much more productive, successful and fulfilled. It is amazing how much connections, thoughts and ideas your brain can be able to accommodate at any given time. There is no limit as to the number of applications you can use mind maps to help you.

## #1 Mind mapping and brainstorming

Brainstorming is a brilliant way of coming up with new ideas and solving problems. It enables you to evaluate the problems from a different perspective, understand the challenges and their root causes, and identify alternative solutions. You can also use brainstorming for decision-making and impact analysis. In the context of project management, you can brainstorm from the goals and objectives, down to the projects to explore new alternatives, ideas, and possibilities. It provides you with a much more complete and understandable plan than the task level planning.

Brainstorming can be particularly great for team building, which involves shared discussions, as well as for individual ideation. It also has the benefit of improving innovation and initiative with an organization, as well as improving profitability and quality, morale and efficiency.

Basic concepts of brainstorming

Basically, brainstorming involves capturing ideas as quickly as possible in order to bypass the judgment you usually use to assess ideas before you record them, and instead capture the ideas as they come up, assuming no time, resource, money or other constraints, without judgment, and build on ideas as they occur as well as pushing yourself to think in new perspectives. The idea is that quality comes out of quantity. There are bound to be great ideas from the pile of ideas you throw in. You should be recording the keywords on topics as you come up with the ideas. When doing this, you don't particularly pay attention to where the topic ends up. However, as long as it is not slowing you down, you can as well group the main topics together, and incorporate related ideas as sub topics. Sometimes it can be useful to have some high-end grouping by placing some of the main topics in their place, and float the topics under your main ideas, creating islands of information that you can refine and organize later on. To help you keep up with the recording, you can simply type the topic, finish by pressing Return/Finish, and then create the next topic by pressing Return/Enter, and so forth. This way, recording the information will be fast as the details come up.

What if you run out of ideas?

Sometimes when brainstorming, you may run out of ideas and are stuck completely, or you may find that there are more ideas related to the main topic than you are already aware of.

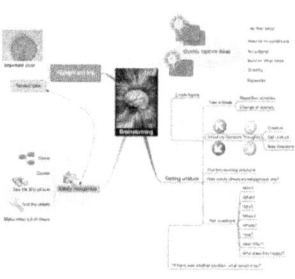

For starters, if you are convinced that there should be more ideas linked to a certain topic, or extra concepts to be derived from the title, include blank topics in your Mind Map, as your subconscious mind does not like to leave things hanging, and will explore new ideas to fill the blank topics.

On the other hand, you can stop what you are doing and take a break by doing something else, or going for a walk. Engaging in a different activity enables your subconscious mind to work on the problem and identify new answers without being under too much pressure. Repetitive activities such as walking are especially great for allowing the thoughts to surface. Changing the scenery like walking by the beach or going to the park can result to a different kind of inspiration where you can think of different ideas. You can decide to take your laptop with you, or something that will enable you to record the ideas as they spring to mind, instead of holding them in your mind until you get to the office.

In most cases when you are thinking about a certain topic, it is not uncommon to be stuck in a loop, where it seems like there is a truck parked in front of the road, and it is very difficult to think of new ideas. This is where it can help to introduce random ideas and words to jolt your memory. It can be helpful to use a thesaurus to first find related words, and then move progressively away from your starting point. At a suitable point, you can then stop and identify the associations back to the initial concept. In some cases, it can be more thrilling to pick a random word from the website or dictionary, and then try relating it to the topic at hand.

Another idea is looking at similar problems in various domains and determining whether you can apply similar solutions that worked in the related domain. It can also help to ask yourself how other people would approach or solve the problem. This is especially useful when taking other parties' perspectives that are involved in the problem, or are affected by the solution. Some of the questions you can ask include:

*Who?

*What?

*How?

*When?

*Why?

*Who does this affect?

*How often?

These questions will encourage you to look at the problem from a different point of view. This idea is based on Neuro Linguistics, and involves putting your imagination into play. It is like acknowledging that there is no other option, but assuming that there was another option just for the meantime, what would it be? And in most cases, your imagination comes into play and provides another idea, and once again, the door that was shutting off ideas opens up.

Once you have recorded enough ideas, you have to organize so that you end up with the general concepts first, followed by the sub topics floating under the main ideas. This will help you see the bigger picture, and the associated details. It is often useful to fix associated topics into floating groups, and then incorporate the floating topic into the mind map. Ensure that the important ideas are highlighted with images or adornments or by color and so on.

Tips and techniques

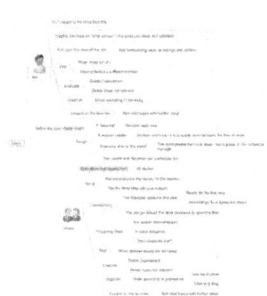

Let explore some important points for brainstorming both by yourself and in a group. The most important thing to do first is to define the topic or problem clearly. The subject should be the title of the Mind Map, and then imagine that you are getting your solutions and ideas from your inner advisor. Start with the top-level topics, followed by the children topics, or floating topics, as needed, without limitation or judgment, and not being concerned about organization. Stop when you have exhausted the ideas, or you have run out of ideas. Once you have enough ideas, you can then organize and evaluate them. Sometimes, you might have to expound the best ideas in the process in order to get more concrete detail.

When you are using mind maps in a group, you need some methods and structures in place to ensure that the entire process goes smoothly. There should be a session leader, a recorder, and everyone else as the panel. It is generally not advisable to have a huge group. Having a group of more than ten to fifteen people can be hard to manage. In this case, it might be convenient to split into several groups, and then incorporate the ideas later on, or reflect on the different aspects of the topic.

Studies have shown that if you start brainstorming with the whole group without first engaging in individual brainstorming, you usually end up with lower quality and fewer ideas. As such, begin by going through the topic identification and the intended purpose with the parties involved to ensure that you are on the same page. Proceed to brainstorm individually before getting back to share the ideas, ensuring that everyone gets a fair say. As you mention and record the ideas on the Mind Map, the ideas related to those topics will come up from the other participants, and these should be put down without constraints or judgment, or elaboration. The point here is to simply get the keywords. The process of elaboration, culling and grouping is pretty much the same as individual brainstorming. Using these techniques, and with this structure in place, you can be able to brainstorm solutions and ideas either in a group or individually, and come up with better ideas and solutions.

Mind mapping is one of the best ways to brainstorm ideas and to arrange the ideas into sensible concepts. A great way to start is to dump your thoughts in a map and then let your imagination run wild as you continue to fill your mind map. Unfortunately, most people who use this technique when brainstorming use it wrongly. Here is how you can use mind maps effectively to brainstorm.

Generally, brainstorming has two phases: divergent thinking and convergent thinking. One common mistake people make while brainstorming is to start with convergent thinking.

The two stages of brainstorming

Before you can develop the ability to create a mind map successfully, it is important to be conversant with the basics. Only then will you be able to use mind maps to brainstorm. The good news is that the process is relatively easy and quite effective.

You need to be aware of the two phases of brainstorming in order to get the most out of these sessions. During the first phase, you and the group generally come up with the topics and ideas you want to cover. This phase is also called divergent thinking. During this stage, you let the ideas flow freely, not thinking about the good and bad stuff, or the semantically correct. At that time, there are no connections or relationships between your thoughts. All the ideas and thoughts are just there as you dump them without judgment. You are basically thinking outside the box at this time and you are not restricted to a framework or set of rules. It is like being a little child who does not understand how the world functions. The child will do whatever they think without being limited to anything and this is exactly the state you want to be in while brainstorming. Convergent thinking is the second phase of brainstorming. At this stage, there is a set of rules governing your options as you try to get the best solution from what you have. This phase is particularly different from divergent thinking where you are allowed to think out of the box. Here, you start organizing your thoughts, map them and then work on finding a solution from the available tangibles. If you relate it to the child analogy at this stage, you have grown up into an adult, you know the rules, and now you want to play under the confines of a set of rules and regulations. If you want to remember this easily, think of the first stage as a matter of quantity over quality; pour out all your thoughts and then represent them using a mind map. Think of the second stage as a matter of quality over quantity. At this stage, you deal with the created thoughts and ideas from the first stage, sieve the thoughts you perceive irrelevant and then organize the remaining information into finding a suitable solution.

#2 Mind mapping and note taking

Picture this scenario. You go into your class as usual, find your lecturer just about to start, so you settle at your desk. As soon as the lecture begins, your mind wanders off, only to recover in the middle of the lesson without a clear view of how everything fits together... This happens to everyone, and in most cases, it is caused by lack of effective study skills that makes us lose concentration and end up assimilating much less information than our brains are capable. This is where you can use Mind Mapping. Mind mapping is an effective technique that improves your learning ability, enhances your method of recording information, and improves and supports creative problem solving. You can easily identify and comprehend the structure of a topic with the help of mind maps. It becomes easy to see how all the pieces of information fit together. In addition, mind maps can also help you remember details since they record the information in your brain in a format that can be easily recalled by your mind. Here are a few tips to use when making notes:

*Be prepared

The first thing you need to do when taking notes is to be fully prepared. If you skip this step, you may end up losing plenty of information that you would have gained.

To start, prepare a mind map with all the information you are already familiar with about the topic. Your mind works by linking new information to the old or existing information. As such, this forms a framework that can be added new information. Expand the mind map by incorporating new topics for the stuff you think or know may be covered. This creates the foundation of concentration for the new information. When this has been achieved, add branches for the topics you want to learn. This will help your mind look out for that information, helping you ask the relevant questions, both to the teacher and to yourself when you are listening to the presentation.

*Color-coding

Various topic shapes can be color coded to represent the various topics. Different software allows you to choose colors that not only rhyme together, but also have brilliant contrast. With these, you can easily color code stuff, as well as have a colorful mind map. One good approach is to set up these topics, and then let the subtopics take up these colors. At the end of the presentation, you can then easily identify the information you were already familiar with at a glance, the information you were expecting and received, and lastly, the answers to your questions.

Taking notes effectively

When in a study session, it is always advisable to add new topics for your existing topics as you learn some new and interesting information. If you can be able to add the topics quickly on the map and position them where they belong, go ahead and do so. However, if you do not have the time for that, do not stress it.

How to memorize the information learnt

The best way to memorize the new information is to review it at progressively advancing intervals, for example one hour, a day, a month and a year. While reviewing the information, you should also include learning to create another copy of the mind map from your mind to ensure you have all the information in your long-term memory. Be sure to use the same colors and topic shapes you used in the original, as this will trigger your mind to recall the association of ideas and words. The best thing about mind mapping is that it makes note-taking feel complete and compact. A whole book summary, lecture, or class can be identified at a glance. It is a brilliantly effective way to comprehend and understand information, study, as well as to review learnt information.

How to create a mind map when taking notes

*Prepare a rough draft: Put together a rough draft quickly. Use printed words, images, and colors to redraft.

\*Create a topic: Find the focus you will be relying on when thinking. Use as few words as possible. Keeping your focal topics simple will help you connect aspects and ideas precisely and in a comprehendible way. On the other hand, a broader subject will make it more tiresome to work with in the future.

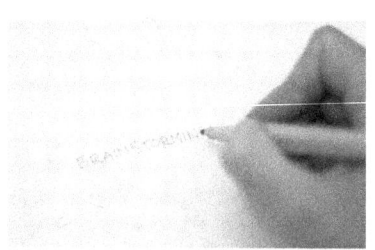

*Position the topic at the center of the page: The idea is to have a visual representation or pictogram of the central topic. Reserve the use of bold letters in topics for things with no plausible visual form.

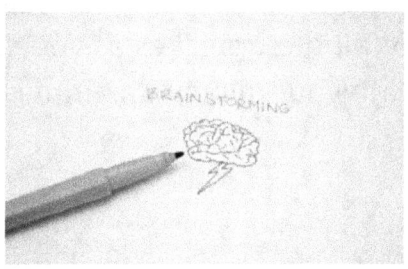

*Size: Your mind map should not exceed an A4 paper. In order to cover more topics, create a mastermind map that will act as a page of contents for different smaller mind maps. Add more paper when needed.

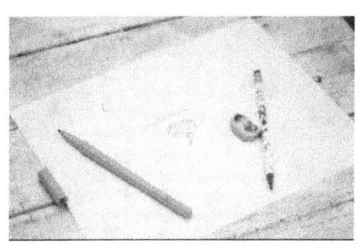

*Use free association to begin the flow of ideas. Write what comes in your mind. Attach branches from the main subject as you generate your thoughts. Minimize your words as much as possible, recording the essentials of all your thoughts succinctly. You can pare the amount of words for all the branches as you continue to populate your mind map. Print clearly.

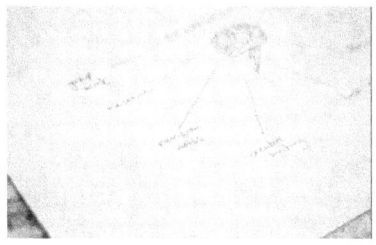

*Choose your words briefly: Record simple phrases or single words.

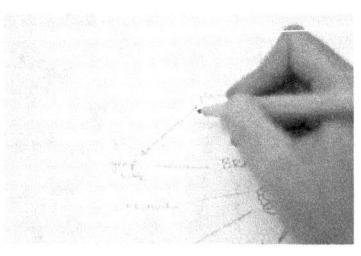

*Continue branching: Branch out of your main topic as you continue studying. Try to expound on your thoughts through different ideas. You can draw lines between your thoughts to encourage lateral thinking.

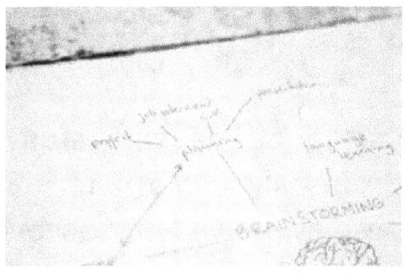

*Draw more branches as you develop new ideas from your topic. Spread out as necessary.

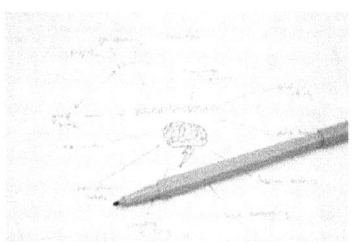

*Continue spreading out until you fill the map with all your ideas.

*When you are done mapping, study the connections carefully and try to refresh their relationships. Have you uncovered any larger patterns?

# Chapter 20: Managing Your Daily Life

" A good relationship with time is one of the signs of a balanced personality that is attentive to others. " **Frank-Louis Servan-Schreiber**

"I haven't done anything good yet today!" " How many times a week do we have the sensation of wasting our time, dissolving ourselves in the insignificant, doing too much in a hurry?

Everyday life and its ever-increasing number of requests make the organization of life laborious: many tasks are to be done at the same time, and we quickly find ourselves "nose in the handlebars" to pedal without knowing too much towards what goal.

The day ends, then leaving a feeling of frustration because the important and priority things have hardly been touched on.

Paradoxically, we would still like to do more and exploit all the good ideas that come to mind (always, obviously, at a bad time).

We then start to mull over a tiring cocktail where trivial and important things mix with urgent tasks. In this state of mind, it becomes difficult to decide where to start.

What about the long term vision? Where are we with respect to our priorities? What is the path already covered on the road to our professional or private goals?

What to do?

This observation of lack of time, we have repeatedly asked and often sought to adopt a method to manage our activity better.

Many people do it empirically: they act "piecemeal" by adding new tasks to the pile of things to do. They favor rewarding and high-performance tasks. Their computer screen is covered with Post-it ®. Their office is tidied up once a month by their assistant. Overwhelmed by the number of things to do, they postpone much of it overnight and no longer have room to manage the unforeseen.

Still, others try the defensive method: staying longer and later in the office when the phone no longer rings, no longer reading their e-mail when each new message arrives. Their doors are often closed, and they use sensory isolation to help them focus on their work. At this point, we started looking for a real recipe table in order to have less " Evil in our time." We read books and magazines or participate in time management seminars without finding the expected answer.

These are not the management methods and systems missing activities: paper agenda, digital assistant, software, or concepts offered by many gurus.

All these methods, as interesting as they are, do not yet completely satisfy us...

We would like to:

- Be available to ourselves and others;

- Distinguish what is important from what is urgent;

- Know what we need to do during the day and when we can say no;

- Visualize what we have achieved according to our objectives;

- Adapt to constantly changing priorities.

The mind map as a piloting tool

This method is implemented very simply by respecting the following steps using a map dedicated to this use: "the star map," which we will use as a compass.

Smith (teacher): "most people ask me how I can have such a full life and how I am able to manage all my activities. I have two tools: the sense of my actions, my reasons for living, and the star card that guides me all day. "

To act

Let's just focus on the highlighted tasks, and the others will be covered later. Our spirit is thus freed, and only the work to be done attracts our full attention. Once a task is finished, we go over it with the other color. The result: a pretty orange color appears instead of pink and yellow.

We see the overall color of the map evolving, which becomes more and more orange as the tasks are carried out. At the end of the day, we take stock: savor our accomplishments and review our priorities for the next day.

Plan

An important step is to identify the time scale with which we will track our work: the month, the week or the day. The week has the following advantages:

• Most of the planning is done once for the week, calm before starting it.

• The scale is wide enough to see the completion of tasks that cannot be done overnight: it is motivating, and it allows postponement until the next day.

• At the end of the week, we take stock of the one that has passed, and we prepare the next one.

The definition of the time scale is an exercise to be redone from time to time and to adapt to your job and circumstances (on vacation, for example, the scale can cover a whole month).

Picking the idea

Organizing your ideas to monitor your activity is a permanent state of mind. Our brain never stops "phosphorizing." The connections, the links between our ideas, are made and unmade according to our occupations, and our objectives to be achieved.

The richest ideas come when you don't expect them. The brilliant idea is often fleeting conjunction of less brilliant ideas. How many times have we had a great idea in the shower, driving the car, in our bed, playing sports, or mowing the lawn? In short, during those moments when the mind wanders more or less freely.

The little thing that makes the difference: pick the idea when it germinates in our mind. Here is a non-exhaustive list of ways to keep the fruits of our imagination:

• a notepad;

• a drawing pad (not for making perfect drawings but for storing embryos of ideas or prototypes);

• a workbook (a lined or grid page for a page of drawing paper);

• a stack of cards in Bristol each illustrated with a logo indicating its purpose: House, Team, Project XYZ;

• colored cards to organize ideas by objectives;

• a Dictaphone ™ or an MP3 player/recorder;

- voicemail: drop ideas on your own voicemail when we have no way of writing them down;

- a camera;

- a block of Post-It ® ;

- a paper desk pad;

- a digital assistant like Palm or Pocket PC ;

- a word processor (from the simple Notepad supplied with Windows to the most sophisticated and its view in "plan" mode to prioritize or classify our ideas);

- software for drawing mind maps (see chapter 8);

- the restaurant tablecloth;

- greeting cards with an integrated chip memorizing 30 seconds of speech;

- while traveling: prepare a series of pre-addressed postcards to send each other the best finds!

Clarify the objectives

The heart of this method consists in acting in coherence with its own objectives. These must be known and refined on a daily basis. The reader will refer to Chapter 2 to deepen the method of defining its objectives. All these loose ideas will serve as material for preparing the star card.

The list is plotted on a draft sheet. It can be interesting to surround it with keywords, to make small drawings illustrating the relationships between our ideas, and to try to see more clearly in our concerns.

This constitutes a real beneficial flattening which helps us to clarify our objectives.

Once this raw list is ready, we can move on to building the star card.

Draw the "star card."

In the center of the page, draw the heart of the card by adding the number of the week in question. This way of proceeding makes it possible to organize a usable archiving thereafter.

Frank: "I use a practical notebook in which drawing paper alternates with normal paper. I draw the star cards on the drawing paper while the normal pages serve as my support to take classic notes or to describe my ideas. I then keep all these notebooks that I classify in chronological order of use during the year."

Starting from the center of the sheet, trace the main branches of the map. They are chosen according to our activity and our objectives.

In this example, we have chosen as main branches: contacts, entertainment, and travel.

By living daily with the star card, we identify our favorite main branches. They are our guidelines and give us a global and representative vision of our work.

By dint of using this method, we give meaning to the colors used in a recurring manner as to the position of our key branches on the diagram.

A STUCE - The "Ideas" branch is used as a reservoir for isolated ideas that do not fail to arise once the star card is activated. Also, provide free space to add the main branch: we remain open to opportunities and changes.

The next step is to complete each of the main branches with the objectives and tasks to be carried out during the week:

Our menu is now ready. We have before us our visual contract for the week to come. We can approach it with confidence because we are sure that we have placed the important and necessary tasks on the map.

Defining our priorities

Planning is done simply with two fluorescent highlighters: a pink for important tasks and a yellow for urgent tasks. At the start of the day, we only highlight the tasks we have to accomplish that day.

Assess

In the past week, we need to plan a moment of calm to review our achievements. It is an important moment that allows us to take stock of the content of our planning, to examine our progress towards our objectives, and to analyze the tasks not carried out.

This evaluation also aims to adopt the following week's scheme to our way of working: identification of new main branches, highlighting our key objectives.

A lived example of a mind map used to organize a weekend is visible in the central insert.

Value-added heuristic map

It is a simple and fun tool to use but with a high added value: we see ourselves progressing with confidence on the paths leading to our objectives.

The star card very quickly becomes an essential "companion" to highlight and organize our daily tasks. Once the card is finished, the pride in the work accomplished provides a feeling of self-control.

We benefit from a global vision of all of our activities. Links and associations are emerging between our tasks.

Frank (e-communication manager): "Since I have been using this method, I can't do without it because it gives a clear vision of my activities! I ended up finding the ideal material (notebook, pen, and highlighters) that I always carry with me. A card is an open tool that allows me to insert new objectives or new tasks at any time to manage the changes, of course, that occur on a daily basis. "

Unlike the many often computerized activity management tools, the star card is inexpensive, available in all circumstances, and reliable. It is enough to use a little paper and a few markers.

## Conclusion

Mind maps are very powerful tools that can help you study, solve problems, take notes and more. They help unlock the full power of your mind to creatively resolve problems, make decisions and help your memory.

A mind map starts with some pens and a piece of blank (not lined) paper that is turned in landscape format, i.e. with the long edge at the top. In the centre of your page you write the main concept that you are mind-mapping about. This needs to be in capital letters and quite a large sized font. If you prefer to include an image here, then that will work very well. You may want to draw a colored circle around this central concept too.

Around this central concept you will write the 'chapter' headings, i.e. the next most important concepts related to the main idea. These are also written in capital letters and can be surrounded by a colored circle or rectangle. These are joined to the main concept by a large, thick line, which indicates the importance of the connection.

Hanging off these you can have a third and fourth level of concepts that you need to mind map about.

The use of colors, shapes and images can help you to create a mind map that activates your brain and helps you to remember everything.

If you want to capture information from a book, seminar or meeting, then mind maps are excellent because they can act as mnemonics. It really helps you recall the information not just afterwards but at any time in the future.

If you need to make a decision or solve a problem, then mapping the information in this way can be really useful tool. The mind map helps you to organize the information so that your brain can absorb it and work to use it to make the decision or come up with a creative solution to the problem.

Some people like to use software to create their mind maps whereas other people prefer to do them by hand. It depends on whether you prefer to draw one by hand or use a computer. Both methods have their pros and cons and it is very much down to you and how you prefer to work.

Whether you are a student who needs to be able to recall information, or someone who needs to keep track of a lot of information or whether you need to make decisions or solve problems you will find that mind maps can help you.

Mind maps are an extremely effective tool to aid recall and problem solving. They can be used by anyone and unlock the creative power of your mind. Working with colors, images and words you use all parts of your mind. The diagrams help you to connect the dots between different concepts and make leaps of judgement and knowledge.

Whatever you are studying, or whatever career you are in, you will find that mind maps are very useful tools that can help you remember facts and solve problems. Learning to use mind maps can make a big difference to your studying and recall and that is something that can only benefit you.

www.ingramcontent.com/pod-product-compliance
Lightning Source LLC
Chambersburg PA
CBHW071433070526
44578CB00001B/90